together
we're
better

by
bev
bos

photographs by michael l. bos
turn the page press

establishing a coactive learning environment

ISBN: 0-931793-01-7
Library of Congress Catalogue Card Number: 90-71653

Edited by Kay Glowes.
Design and Graphics by Michael L. Bos.
Illustrations by Michael J. Leeman.
Printed at Delta Lithograph

To Bob and my children and grandchildren, as well as all the children, parents, and teachers of the Roseville Community Preschool.

A particular thanks to Tom Hunter for allowing me to use the lyrics of his song as my title.

contents

introduction

Tremendous growth in the base of early childhood research and our corresponding ability to apply this knowledge in the education of our children should be making it easier for early childhood teachers to function as they know they should. But I cannot say that this is what I see in the schools I visit across the country. I believe that pressure to ignore or neglect the needs of young children is increasing, rather than decreasing. Although I have made the particular focus of this book social development in the young child, I want to begin my discussion in the context of continuing attempts to force premature growth in young children.

I believe that all teachers know what good programs are and believe they should provide them, but throughout the country opposing pressure from parents, principals, directors, and trustees for inappropriate programs seems to be not only continuing but increasing. Nearly every night of the week, I give a workshop on how to put together better programs for young children. At nearly every workshop I listen to teachers afraid, sad, often literally in tears because they are horrified at what is happening to children in classrooms and feel powerless to prevent it. Last year I presented workshops in twenty states, and while I hear many wonderful, exciting reports and see many excellent

Sooner is not better. Faster is not better.

programs for young children, I hear all too many tragic stories and see entirely too many programs that will stunt the growth of young children or, even worse, damage them forever as learners and human beings.

Why? I believe that many parents and administrators have childhood amnesia. Most adults do not remember being two, three, four, or five years old—and if they do, they have painful and isolated memories. They want their children's lives to be better, but too many seem have no way of identifying what "better" might be—except more of everything faster and sooner—unless we as teachers make it clear to them that sooner is not better, faster is not better.

Research has demonstrated not only that there are predictable stages of growth in children, but that since all children are unique, a good program for young children must be responsive to individual differences. Development, after all, refers simply to stages of growth.

But the word *developmental* has gotten a bad name, sending up red flags to parents, who seem to feel that a teacher recommendation for a developmental program is a statement that a child is slow and not ready for "real" school—whatever that is. Many teachers have commented on this problem, but none more clearly than former president of the National Association for the Education of Young Children Docia Zavitkowsky, who reminds us that what we should be doing, rather than trying to get children ready for school, is to get schools ready for children.

At the start of each new school year, we have an orientation in which we present every aspect of our early childhood program. We talk about how young children learn. I tell our parents that I care about them and their children—deeply. I will do everything and anything to help them grow and learn together. But the one thing I will not do is teach their children in an inappropriate way. We will prepare an environment to enable children to learn and grow at their own rates and in their own ways, but we will not have a curriculum based on only one aspect of a child's development.

Last year after orientation at our school, a father stayed to talk. He had visited another early childhood program in our area. The teacher was teaching letters of the alphabet to one or two children at a time, while other children waited, lined up with their backs against the wall.

When he told the teacher that he had done a good deal of reading in early childhood growth and development and believed that this was inappropriate curriculum, she agreed with him completely. But she said that parental pressure had made her succumb to this style of teaching. She truly resented the pressure and the necessity to give in to it, she said. But what, we ask, about fairness and educational justice for these children?

Another sad story: a young teacher told me one night after a workshop that she had done her studies in early childhood education under many recognized masters in the field, but that she had finally given in

"Rather than getting children ready for school, we need to get school ready for children."

--Docia Zavitkowsky

If we don't, who will?

to parental pressure and was teaching inappropriate material, using worksheets, a practice contrary to everything she had been taught. I recently heard that she has abandoned her teaching.

What is the answer? First, we ourselves, as teachers, must know the research. It is no longer enough for us to say we "think" it is best to individualize instruction and to pay attention to stages of development. Then we must educate—parents, principals, program directors, trustees. I believe that when early childhood education first came into its own, many people were hired for positions they had not been adequately educated for. Entirely too many people in positions of influence have little or no background in early learning. We must try to be understanding of these failings, but that does not mean we can give up on educating everyone to fundamentally sound approaches to the education of young children. As teachers of young children, we must become advocates for developmentally appropriate learning in our homes, classrooms, and schools. If we don't, who will?

Here is a brief set of situations based on presenting opportunities for social growth in young children. I do not necessarily suggest that you ask these questions of your parents or boards of directors. Instead, read the questions yourself as a gauge. How developmentally appropriate are practices in your school? Do they remain appropriate even when they come into conflict with the parental and administrative attitudes I have just been discussing? Suggested answers and my discussion are given on page 24.

(1) A teacher has just started reading a story to twenty young children. A child jumps up and interrupts, shouting, "Stop! This is the best story, and I want Charles to hear it!" What should the teacher do?

(a) Remind the interrupting child that it is story time and ask her to sit down; (b) ask an assistant or aide to remove the child; (c) wait for the child to go and get Charles so that he can hear the story; (d) quietly shush the interrupting child by putting a finger to her lips.

(2) A four-year-old boy is having a difficult time separating from his mother. He has said his goodbyes, and she has reassured him about the time she will return. The teacher has quietly comforted him. He cries at the door, walks through the school crying, and cries his way outside, where he finds a good friend. "You have to stay by me and play with me," he tells the friend.

"I'm no fool," the friend responds. "I'm not going to play with somebody who's crying all the time."

What should the teacher do?

(a) Gently direct the friend to play with the crying child; (b) try to find another friend for the crying child; (c) pick the crying child up and console him with toys or a swing; (d) step back and see if the four-year-old can handle this himself.

(3) In our school we have several lofts. I always say the loft areas remind me of the loges in a movie theater. From the loft the children can hear the songs we sing during group time and see and hear the

story books being read, and there are three or four children who prefer, especially at the beginning of the year, to stay up in the loges and look down. Usually they are quiet, but occasionally they will shout out an answer or a question. Should I insist they join the rest of the children during group time?

(4) It is music time and the activity requires that everyone get a partner. Most of the children grab another's hand and are ready to go, but a few hang back with their fingers in their mouths, eyes downcast, partner-less. What should the teacher do?

(a) Take the child's hand and find another child who doesn't have a partner; (b) become the child's partner; (c) ignore the situation and let the child sit this one out; (d) pick partners for all the children at the beginning of the week so no child has to risk doing this; (e) glance around the room and say, "Sarah, John doesn't have a partner and neither does Julie," or "Sarah, see if Julie and Jimmy will let you join them."

See page 24 for suggested answers and my discussion.

coactivity: what and why?

I have always believed that as parents and educators, we need to be concerned with the whole child—the social, emotional, intellectual, physical, spiritual child. But after giving more than three thousand workshops and hearing the questions people have about how to be with children, I find one of the questions that continues to be most often asked is how to encourage socialization.

This book has thus developed out of my particular concerns for the child who has not yet become socially competent. It comes from observations in my own preschool as well as from listening carefully to other adults—both educators and parents—about concerns for that aspect of the whole child that we might call the *social* child.

Many books on cooperative games and cooperative learning are already available to parents and educators; I have included some of them in the bibliography of this book. Why write still another book about socialization? And why call it coacting?

I believe it is especially important to distinguish between concepts of cooperating and coacting in thinking about programs and activities for the young child. I am using the word *coacting* here rather than *cooperating*, as I did in my second book, *Before the Basics*, to distinguish between *cooperative* situations, in which several participants act in an organized way toward an end and *coacting* situations, in which participants more often simply act together in a spontaneous way, action I believe more appropriate to the young child.

Thus *cooperating* implies a mutually recognized goal, but in *coacting*, a more spontaneous process, a goal is not required. *Coaction* is simply a way of interacting with others, more often one-on-one than in larger groups, with an emphasis on process rather than product. I believe that developing coaction skills is a necessary foundation for developing cooperating skills—a set of skills which comes at a later developmental stage.

Continuing to group all our ideas about socializing under the heading of cooperation—a skill that does not come easily at any age and a skill that teachers realize is probably developmentally impossible for most young children--can unfortunately lead us to gloss over coaching as a necessary base for more advanced social competencies. I am my own best example here: in working out the details of my own program, I have needed to clarify this distinction for myself. This clarifying process has made me realize that although the distinction between coaction and cooperation seems terribly obvious in hindsight, it is a distinction that is much lacking in the everyday, practical reality of how we deal with children in social environments.

As teachers, probably we don't even think very much about planning daily activities for young children in terms of cooperating. Our intuition and experience put us on the right track here. The very young

One of the single clearest—and most delightful—examples of the three-year-old yearning for group play, but not yet ready for full participation, was Andy, who watched himself one day to the fringes of a group of older children playing family. He watched and watched, silently, as they distributed roles--mother, father, brothers, and sisters--and played out their game. Finally, one of the older children noticed him and came over and invited him to join. "We need a dog," the older child said, and Andy happily joined, still entirely silent, lying down, occasionally panting, allowing himself to be patted on the head.

child is no more ready to engage in daily demands to cooperate than to do higher order mathematics.

Research supports our informal belief. The social life of an infant (birth to eighteen months) is conducted primarily with adults rather than with other children.. At ages two and three, children generally engage in parallel play—playing close to a group but essentially by themselves. Even in day-care centers, two-year-olds play by themselves, often paying no attention to others in the same room. Two-year-olds may begin to be onlookers, observing others, but not getting involved. Three-year-olds move into the next stage slowly, often engaging in parallel play, but also beginning at times to be quite social. The four- or five-year-old will begin to display much more associative and cooperative play

It is during these preschool years that I believe it is crucial to encourage coactive play by establishing appropriate environments and understanding what can be expected developmentally from young children.

For example, don't expect three-, four-, and five-year-olds to want to share their possessions. Given time and a coactive environment, sharing will develop naturally.

You will be able to find many fine discussions of developmentally appropriate behaviors and activities for young children. For example, the National Association for the Education of Young Children has published a fine set of guidelines edited by Sue Bredenkamp: *Developmentally Appropriate Practice in Early Childhood Programs Serving*

Children from Birth Through Age 8 (1987). The book can be purchased from the NAEYC, 1834 Connecticut Avenue, N.W., Washington, DC 20009-5786.

Why be concerned? Several years ago, I began to become worried about the number of children leaving us for kindergarten or first grade who were not yet socially competent.

I am not, of course, contending that all children are equal in social skills. Of course, they are not. But by the age of five, although all children are still egocentric and will find it difficult to be empathetic, all children should be able to belong—to fit into a small group. Many children are quiet—but socially competent. Other children are boisterous and assertive—but socially competent. Social competence in any child is the ability to coact, make friends, speak up when one likes or doesn't like something, argue and and then return to peers.

It is very painful to see a child having trouble belonging. We need to remember that it is even more painful for the child. Children are born needing to belong—first to a family, then to a school, a community, the world. Belonging is sharing emotions and intelligence, being comforted, accepted, and encouraged, being part of a spiritual and cultural tradition and accepting the traditions of others. Belonging is sharing, sharing a part of ourselves and our homes, families, and cultures. Essentially, together we are all better.

How well we are able to express our-selves and our needs, our concerns to others will be a deciding factor in our success or failure as human beings.

How well we are able to express ourselves and our needs, our concerns to others will be a deciding factor in our success or failure as human beings. How well we develop socially will have an effect on our lives forever.

As I focused on some of our children at kindergarten age who still did not know how to make friends, how to become part of a group, I saw two extremes of behavior: the child who still pushed and shoved to get attention and, at the other extreme, the child who was completely withdrawn.

We all recognize both these children. The first will be a high-energy child, often very articulate, who can't go into a small group without antagonizing other children. This child is often physically aggressive. What happens? Other children push this child away. The teacher, if the teacher succumbs to a time-out solution, pushes this child away. By kindergarten or first grade, this child will be isolated by the school itself through suspension processes. We can see tragic patterns beginning for this child as early as the preschool.

No less potentially tragic is the child whose parent comes in and says, "This is James. He's shy." Then everyone overreacts, using the word "shy," every time James has any kind of interaction with other children or with the program. It is very likely that James will become increasingly withdrawn as he fails to develop his own skills and as other children perceive him as unable to join a group or to interact with other children. As we all know, without the right kind of attention, these behaviors will not improve with time. Socializing becomes increasingly difficult because the child has not learned established responses. As other children begin to form their own friendships, the child who has not been given an opportunity to learn social skills is left out, reinforcing behaviors that appear still more antisocial as other children develop.

It was out of my concerns for both these types of children that I began to examine the environment in our school and to ask myself if and how we could change that environment to better help children socialize. Could we, in some very natural ways, get one child closer to another? In particular, could we encourage both the over-aggressive child and the overly quiet child to interact positively with others while accomplishing other developmental tasks—and without calling attention to the process?

In working out an approach, I soon began to realize, of course, that all our children would benefit immensely from some conscious attention to coacting. It is our job as adults to establish coactive environments which allow children's natural abilities to develop and then to step back and trust children to help each other, work together, converse, dream aloud, make friends, and simply learn how to be in their worlds. Not just the target child, but all our children will gain.

In setting up these learning environments, we need to begin by asking a series of questions pointed toward socialization components: Can this activity be done by one child successfully, but does it also encourage a child to ask another to help? Does this activity automatically require two children? Can we expand this individual project to include more children? Can we make this learning environment non-competitive?

As we begin to create a total environment at home or within the school that will allow children to maximize positive social behaviors at their own rates and by their own choice, we will find it less and less necessary to focus on extremes of behavior. I have organized this book as an alphabet of coactivity to discourage thinking about coactivity as part of only certain activities and programs within the school. Coactivity is a set of building blocks, quite literally an alphabet out of which we could desirably spell out our entire program for children.

Thus my purpose in writing this book is to give suggestions about how to incorporate coactive learning into all areas of early childhood programs as well as at home and in neighborhood play groups. In the following chapters I will offer a coactivity checklist, some *dos* and *don'ts* for establishing a coactive environment, and my own alphabet of coactivity, out of which I have every confidence you will be able to build your own.

a coactivity checklist

T he more I think about coaching, the easier it becomes to handle difficult situations. Every day I examine what works for our children—going over the events of each day, thinking about children that are socially competent, asking how this competence was achieved, thinking about the child who has struggled and is finally making it, trying to think of activities that seem to work with almost all children.

I have developed a checklist that I use so regularly that I feel the questions are written on my forehead. Some of the things you will read in this checklist seem to apply to situations beyond coacting, but I decided to include some additional thoughts about individual problems because of the many questions I get in workshops about teacher concerns for a particular child. At any rate, here's my checklist. I invite you to use it, add to it, make it your own, and make it a way of teaching life.

(1) How many times today did I have to help a child solve a social problem? What kind of problems were they? Was this the same child I helped yesterday?

When you have helped solve a social problem, which solutions worked and which did not? Sometimes we have heard or read that

When two children work and play together, conversations happen that adults cannot begin to understand. Children speak to each other in a special language.

there is a particular solution to a certain problem, and without thinking, we begin to make it our number one solution. Time out, for example, has become a popular method of taking care of a child with a problem. Certainly it works for the moment. I do not believe it changes a child's behavior.

I want children to coact because it feels better, because it is more fun to do things together, and because it is more fun to talk things over. One of the problems with time out in our school, for example, is that there really is no place for children to sit where others can't see them, and use of time out thus humiliates a child—a violation of what I consider the most important rule in working with young children—never, never humiliate them. Obviously, time out isn't for us.

In contrast, I believe time out works pretty well at home. Sometimes parents and children need just a few minutes to cool off. Often what children need when they are very angry is simply to move—to run or walk very fast to expend some of that energy of anger. How many of you have been able to clean the whole house in just five minutes when you were really angry?

One of the things we do when a child is having a difficult time is simply to take the child for a walk. We don't talk. We don't lecture. We just walk. Then after the child has calmed down, we listen to the child.

And we don't argue about what has happened. After all, at this egocentric age, the child will see only one side of the story. After we listen, we have a conversation if it seems necessary. Sometimes, I gently and quietly go over the rules. Use words. "People are not for hitting." Then we go back into the classroom. This kind of help for the child is possible because we have parents helping in the classroom.

A wonderful thing happened last year. When his mother enrolled Michael, she said, "He has a terrible temper, and I feel sorry for you. We can't do anything with him."

Sure enough, he had a terrible temper. We tried lots of different things, and when Michael was very, very angry, we would take him for a walk. Michael made more and more friends, and socializing became easier for him. But one day, he came marching into the school in a very bad mood and said, "Hey, someone take me for a walk before I hit one of these kids." We took him for a walk, and he cried a little, and then finally said: "Okay. Wipe my nose so I can go back, and we do not need to talk either."

Imagine a four-and-a-half-year-old understanding himself that well! Many adults have days when they couldn't do half as well.

(2) How much of my time is spent enforcing rules? Could I change the environment in a way that would limit rule making? Have I established an environment that encourages children to work together?

(3) How often do I give directions to the whole group? How often are directions given with children sitting at desks or tables?

Children should be able to come into school and immediately go to a center which is almost entirely self-explanatory. I see the teacher as a

We seem to have such good sense about children when they are babies: we marvel at their every ability. When they crawl, we clap and cheer. When they try to clap and cannot quite connect their hands, we laugh and continue to clap. Why does the cheering for trying stop? Why does it change to cheering only for winning?

facilitator rather than a director. For example, we have attached Duplo® boards to the walls of our lofts. No child needs to be told how to attach Duplo® blocks to the boards. Playdough should be set out with lots and lots of cutters, old scissors, and rolling pins, and children should run to that center. When children arrive at school, the room should be alive with things to do.

(4) How much emphasis am I putting on keeping a tight schedule?

I remember my horror as a child when a teacher kept a rigid schedule every day. Sometimes it seemed to me that I was just beginning to understand something when we had to stop and begin something else. Schedules need to be general and for everyone's benefit.

I have a schedule: the children come at 9:00 a.m., and they leave at ll:30 a.m. They have free time from 9:00 to 10:15 or 10:30. There are lots of small group things that happen during that time, and often our children make their own snack.

Some teachers ask if our children help in planning. They are planning all the time—what to build, what to paint, what colors to use to repaint the fort.

(5) How many times today did I catch myself saying one child's name over and over in a disciplinary way?

We all do this. I am ashamed to tell you that every year I have a child who falls into this category. What I do to solve the problem is this—and I don't wait until April to try.

If what we want for our children is a lifetime of excellence--in experience, ability, knowledge--we must be responsible enough to wait for and thorough enough to consider-- all sides of their development.

I have a schedule: the children come at 9:00 a.m., and they leave at ll:30 a.m.

I go home, and in a quiet spot I take a sheet of paper and a pen and number from one to ten and write down ten positive things about this child—endearing, wonderful, admirable things. I push myself to do ten: five is easy. Sometimes I jot down solutions that come to me.

Let me tell you what I wrote about Duncan this year:

(a) High energy. He is the child that often will be the runner when others are building or painting outside. He uses his energy in a positive way.

(b) Extremely articulate. Duncan can explain how he feels. He can explain in great detail what happened at the grocery store two weeks ago. I need to have him write these stories down, tell them to other children.

(c) Loves to build. Another way to use energy.

(d) Incredibly well-coordinated. We need to help him build obstacle courses and challenging ways to climb.

(e) Loves to laugh and play jokes on others.

(f) Likes smaller children and loves to help them.

(g) Likes to listen to stories, especially from the loft. That's okay.

(h) Likes to paint but wants to be outside. We need to take the art outside for this child.

(i) Amazingly sensitive to other children's feelings. Will say to me, "Laura is sad today." I ask, "Did you find out why?" "No! But I will."

(j) Likes me a lot. His smile in the morning is worth everything.

I'll tell you frankly that this is a child that could drive me to distraction with concern. But I focus on the positive and what Duncan can do and how I can help him do it. I still have to shake my head at him from across the room sometimes, but we are getting there. And Duncan is going to go on in the world and he will make it. He will not drop out. He will get attention for the positive things he does.

(6) Today, how many of the activities I planned were put together with the idea that they could be done not only by one child but could include another child? Did the activities I planned encourage children to ask each other to help or participate in the activity?

Never let a day go by without reflecting on what is important for children. I drive my staff to distraction with new ideas. Sometimes I call them from across the country to tell them a new idea. I am always questioning what I do. Often the questioning comes from deep concern over one child. That, of course, is what has impelled me to write this book: concern for each child.

Answers

See page 4 for questions.

(1) C. Imagine the coaction when Susie tells Charles that this is a wonderful story. The teacher could say ten times that this is a wonderful story, but children know that teachers always think their stories are wonderful. In this case, Susie guided Charles to the circle and made room for him. It is interesting that the two had not been particularly good friends. The teacher should thank Susie and welcome Charles.

(2) D. What actually happened in this situation was that the crying child wiped his eyes after a few minutes and said, "Well, I guess I'll have a better time if I'm not crying." Certainly this happy ending won't occur all the time, and sometimes a teacher must resort to distracting a child, but if we always take care of children's social lives, they will never learn that they are capable of taking over.

(3) No. Emphatically, no. Young children get involved and pay attention to what is interesting to them. If we go about the business of using stories and songs that include children, they will come around. I have never lost a child to the loft.

(4) E. This is a sticky situation, and it is often hard to know what to do, but I would advise E as preferable. The ultimate goal, of course, is to have children feel confident enough socially to reach out for partners. It takes a long time for some children to feel that confident: it may never happen if we always save children by becoming their partners. In the last analysis, we need to give this kind of situation our best and then go with the activity. Some children will need to sit it out. I believe it is genuinely important not to focus attention on children who hang back, but to make them as responsible as possible for their own social lives.

ten dos and don'ts of coactivity

Don't hover.

As adults, we sometimes feel, incorrectly, that we can socialize for our children. Because we are in control of children's environment, we want to create positive social experiences for our children, to prevent our children from being taken advantage of, to support them when they need guidance. But we must not forget that no one can socialize for another human being.

In trusting young children to make their own social choices, we help them develop self-trust and encourage social independence. If we always pick and choose our children's friends, our children will not learn to trust themselves to make these choices, and they will become socially dependent on us. We can't save them every time they experience a painful social interchange, but we can help them to develop the skills they will need to make better choices. Children must eventually be responsible for their own social lives.

At the same time, and even more important, I want to communicate how important it is for parents and educators to establish an environment that encourages socializing without demanding it. Too often, I observe children being put into purposefully arranged groups of four or five and moved from learning center to learning center every fifteen minutes. It is difficult for anyone to learn anything in fifteen minutes, but it is very difficult, perhaps impossible, for young children to socialize, to get to know one another at all, when they are being moved by an adult at this rate—and all too often, I might add, for the purpose of separating friends.

I see conflicts between children as opportunities to guide them towards social competence. In a coactive environment I find that discipline means self-discipline as children are given space to work things out for themselves. They learn to trust and respect each other, and the need for adult intervention decreases.

Each child has a personal timetable, and we need to trust that each child will develop to an individual potential at that personal rate. If you have established a child-centered, developmentally appropriate program, then you should be able to stand back, observe that timetable, and respect it.

The more child-centered your program is, the less you will have to prepare and direct. This is especially true when your concern is coacting. The more we hover and direct social activity, the less it develops in a natural way. With young children, there has to be an adult present to pick them up, dust them off, comfort them, and send them on their ways, but we have to be careful that our presence does not intrude. If our goal for our children is social competence, then we need to trust their inherent ability to socialize and their sense of power

No child ever learned anything in fifteen minutes. We often provide small amounts of tempera and water for paint mixing experiences. Arthur went immediately to that table when he arrived at 9:00 a.m., and at 9:55 he was still mixing. He made almost two quarts of brown paint. The next day when he arrived, he was barely inside when he announced to the whole school: "I know how to get brown!" He didn't mix paint the rest of the school year.

in relationships—not power over someone else, but their power over and for themselves.

We want children to learn how to choose and how to assert themselves appropriately within relationships. This power does not develop in the shadow of adult interference. Today's single-child family could benefit by considering and attempting to imitate one of the principal benefits of the large family of past generations: the opportunity to learn social skills by practicing them without adult interference. When I was a child, my mother fed and clothed us, took care of our physical needs, and then sent us out the back door. There were eight of us. My mother and father were there when we needed a Band-aid™ or a little comfort, but our parents didn't have time to be our social directors or referees. We quickly learned that inappropriate social behavior left us out. We took care of each other; we fought, negotiated, bargained. We learned the skills of socializing by using these skills without adults hovering over our every move.

After observing young children for thirty years, I know that children get involved and stay involved in all that is interesting to them. While we can sometimes encourage children to become interested in new things, we must be careful not to usurp children's freedom to choose their own activities and the peers with whom they will do those activities. I am deeply concerned about adults scheduling every minute of a young child's life with organized lessons and activities. If our eagerness to enrich our children's experiences leads to this kind of overloading, we can accomplish exactly the opposite of what we want to happen. We prevent our children from discovering for themselves those activities and peers they most enjoy.

When school begins, I set up an environment that encourages children to seek out others when they need help. While sitting in circle the first day or two, I talk about how many of us are new and how we don't always remember everyone's name and how frightening it can be when we need help. I tell them if they just call, "Friend, friend," someone will hear them. We practice a little. Often, I hear it during the ensuing weeks: "Friend, friend! I need help!" Does it always work? Good heavens, no! But it plants seeds of cooperative play.

We have somehow gotten the idea that every child must do something in every area of a center every day. In some programs, for example, children must each day finish an art project, do something at the science table, participate in a music program, and play outside for a designated length of time. This adult over-structuring blocks co-active learning.

Adult over-structuring blocks coactive learning.

Don't be afraid of silence.

When I read a story or a poem or when I am singing with children, I value their interruptions. The most important thing to me is what each child thinks is going to happen or how children could change a song, a poem, or a story to suit themselves. The most difficult aspect of doing this is waiting and waiting and waiting for a child to answer.

If we want children to learn to respect the ideas and opinions of others, we must act as models for them. Someone once told me that most teachers wait only a half-second before they jump in with an answer to help a child who is hesitating. I must unfortunately conclude that this is probably so. Grocery shopping, I recently met a child who was in our school last year. I asked her how things were going at school. She said, "It's the funniest thing! My teacher asks a question, and she never waits for the answer!"

I believe that I have all day to wait—and if I fail to wait, if I interrupt the child I have called on, other children will observe the embarrassment of the first child and hesitate to volunteer. If we are to involve all children, and if our concerns are particularly for children who seem unsure of themselves, we must value that moment of silence.   Children learn to pay attention to each other by our modeling of patience and respect for them.

There is another kind of silence perhaps even harder for adults to observe. Folk musician Tom Hunter, who composed the song that is the source of my title for this book, tells a wonderful story that he calls "The Girl Who Sang Her Own Songs."

"When we were members of a parent co-op nursery school in San Francisco, I would go now and then to take my turn as teaching parent.
My favorite thing to do was sit in the play area and watch the children. Some would play together easily. Some needed help. Some liked being alone.   Some were loud and moved fast, others quiet and slower.   Some were particular about what they did, some more slapdash.

"One girl fascinated me because she would sit by herself, swing gently on the swing set, and make up wonderful songs about her day. With no identifiable tune, she'd sing things like

'Today I got up and brushed my teeth,
And my mom gave me cereal for breakfast,
And then I got dressed and got in Aunt Jane's carpool
   to come to school,
And my best friend is Melissa.'

Look, Ma, I'm thinking!   I had told the children during circle that day to pay attention to a child who was thinking. Danielle was obviously impressed. She told her mother and father at dinner that evening that Teacher Bev had taught her how to think. They were suitably intrigued and asked her how . Danielle put her head back and rolled her eyes to the left and to the right.

Together, Hand in Hand

© 1989
Tom Hunter

By our·selves we're good, but to·ge·ther we're
By our·selves we sing, but to·ge·ther we

bet·ter, to·ge·ther were much bet·ter hand in
(sing) bet·ter, to·ge·ther we sing bet·ter hand in

hand. CHORUS:There are big hands, lit·tle hands,
hand.

wa·ving hands and clap·ping hands, all dif·ferent

kinds of hands to·ge·ther hand in hand.

Additional verses :

By ourselves we can work, but together we work better...

By ourselves we can play, but together we play better...

By ourselves we can laugh...

By ourselves we can cry...

--once-in-a-lifetime ballads—straightforward, informative, often very creative. She'd sing as she sat on the swing facing into the big part of the play area where most of the activity was, happy to sing and create on her own.

"I liked to stand nearby and listen. One day on an impulse to encourage her, I told her, 'I really like your songs.' She smiled and said thanks, but she also stopped singing. A parent reported to me that she didn't sing the next day either nor the next. She was also no longer facing into the big part of the play area but had turned around on the swing and was now facing toward the fence away from the activity. Her music had stopped. For three weeks she was quiet and faced the fence. Then someone told me that she was again facing toward most of the kids, and she was again singing songs."

Sometimes our efforts to encourage someone are stifling instead of encouraging. Sometimes, even with the best of intentions, we inhibit creativity. Sometimes it's best just to listen and notice and leave well enough alone.

Why do we feel we have to comment on every piece of art and every ball of playdough rolled into nothing? Why do we feel we must find something to say about the way two children are playing together?

Better than interrupting, with comments, is the written validation, to be taken home, providing a non-intrusive way of acknowledging a child's social and program successes. When a child goes home and is asked by a parent, "What did you do today?" a negative experience is often uppermost in the child's mind; but with a validation in hand, a

Validations need to be specific. Praise a specific action of the child. Simply to write that the child is "wonderful" doesn't say much and puts enormous pressure on the child to be wonderful all the time. Say instead, "Dear Taylor: Thank you for helping Shauna."

positive experience will be relived and discussed, and positive social behavior will be reinforced.

Themes are to live out or play out—not just to talk about.

Don't allow a rigid curriculum or disciplinary methods to narrow possibilities for social interaction.

We can prevent interaction between children when our planned curriculum is restrictive and exclusive. The child is the curriculum. Children do not learn in "units," and all curriculum should be integrated.

For the sake of our own planning, we often use a thematic approach. We must be sure themes are relevant to the child's world: themes are to live out or to play out—not just to talk about. For example, the winter holidays are always very exciting for children. I see a tendency to put the holidays away too quickly, often before the children are through with the costumes, the hats, the books, and the songs. Suppose they need to talk about it just a little more? Especially to each other? When children are being self-directed and genuinely excited, their excitement will almost always include other children, establishing just the social environment we are trying to promote.

Pajama Week continues to be one of the most successful themes we use in our school. One year, a child wore his pajamas to school a week in advance. He told us he was just practicing for Pajama Week!

My guide for packing a theme away is three days having gone by without anyone bringing the theme up: even then, I would retrieve any item a child asked for. Would you turn down the child who comes to you in March bursting with excitement with a request for a Hallow-een book?

Our flexibility and willingness to follow a child's lead will allow remarkable things to happen, if we let them.

Being too literal with our curricula is not the only way we can narrow possibilities. When there is difficulty with children and the first thing a teacher thinks of is "discipline," everyone's in trouble. When difficult situations arise in my school, I don't just jump in with a method of discipline. I try not to separate children but to give them the tools to negotiate. For example, John and Jacob were riding tricycles on the circular bike trail and met, tire-to-tire. They were both absolutely sure of having the right-of-way and each was equally sure he should not have to be the one to move. After observing them for ten seconds, I knew there was going to be a physical confrontation unless I stepped in.

Kneeling down at their level, I listened to both of them tell me the same thing: "I was here first. He has to move." I said, "John, Jacob wants you to move. Jacob, John wants you to move. We have a problem. I want you to give me three ways to solve the problem."

Finally, they came up with three suggestions. An initially hostile situation became friendly as they tried to work together. Jacob finally said, "Oh, well. I'll just back up."

Give children the tools to negotiate.

I believe the same criticism might be made of time-out as a method. While time-out is better than physical punishment, it is not a productive method of dealing with children. Time-out ends behavior for the moment, but doesn't change it. The disruptive child wants to play with other children but doesn't know how. What's the solution? Not isolation, but communication. We must establish and teach guidelines. We've got to tell other children how to deal with high-energy peers and tell this child how to deal with others.

Do mix it up: no chairs, no lines, no tape.

When you are setting up the environment, ask yourself how you can arrange things to get one child next to another. Our easels, for example, are attached to the wall at ninety-degree angles to each other. There is plenty of room to move, but children are thus close enough to talk.

Establish lofts or platforms, which can be built even in the smallest rooms, where children can be close to each other. Recently two fathers in our school built benches that hold two children, and soon we will have no chairs at all. All children will have to sit next to each other on benches.

When I first started teaching, I used to have the children bring chairs to circle and place them on a taped line. Now I encourage the children to sit on the floor all over each other. They learn about others and the space that belongs to others, and they meet children they didn't know before.

In some schools, I have seen lines drawn in the yard to direct tricycle traffic. How will our children learn about head-on traffic and roadway communication if they are never allowed to meet each other head-on? Remember John and Jacob.

Do move it.

The more we restrict movement, the more we restrict the ability of the child to develop socially. I refer here not only to movement by the child but to movement of items within the environment. "A place for everything and everything in its place" is a wonderful thought for adults, but in the best learning environments for children, things must be moved. Allowing movement encourages coactive play. It's difficult to move without connecting with someone else, and it's even more difficult to move things by yourself.

Just today, for example, a child hauled four or five pieces of lumber upstairs to the playhouse area. My first inclination was to step in and say, "You may build with wood outside." What stopped me was the determined look on the child's face: I knew that for some reason not immediately apparent to me, taking the lumber upstairs was very important to him. What happened? Several other children followed suit. They put houses, buildings, boats together. Then they wanted to glue them together. Some children became "runners" to get supplies that others needed. One child who has had difficult coaching became totally involved as a supplier. Thank goodness I did not let my adult instincts interfere with an understanding of what's important in a social environment for children.

A. entry hall
B. baths and storage
C. texture table
D. science and nature
E. puzzle table
F. cut and color table
G. loft
H. swing
I. rocking chair
J. bookshelves
K. block room and dress-up
L. train table
M. loft
N. blocks
O. stairs
P. easels
Q. art table
R. sink
S. art supplies
T. kitchen and office

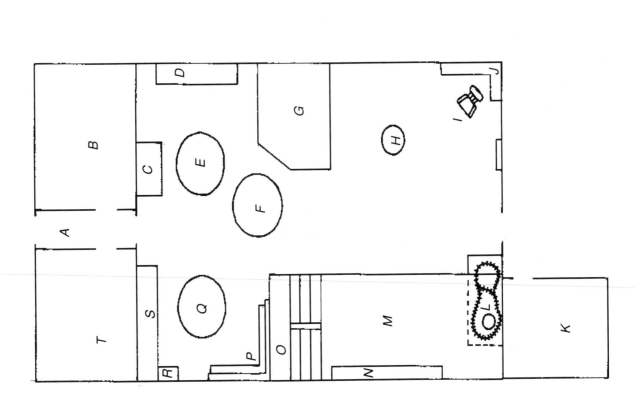

Do hang on to your sense of humor.

Sometimes the most trying situations can be put into perspective by even one person keeping a sense of humor. Children are not born with a sense of humor. If we can teach them by our example how to laugh in the middle of a confrontation—not at others, but at the situation or at themselves, we will have succeeded in communicating one of the most important lessons of social interaction.

Sometimes, I'm happy to say, they demonstrate a capacity to return the favor. One day our children were all playing with the hose, and Doug got sprayed. He came running in to protest: "Somebody got me all wet!!"

There was dead silence for about ten seconds. Then Doug said, "Hey! I just remembered!! I like to be wet!!" And he burst out laughing.

Do respect individual timetables.

I believe it takes everyone a lifetime to become socially competent. Often adults express concern for the "shy" child. I have come to object very strongly to that word. While it is true that some children are quieter than others and that some children seem to make friends quickly while others struggle, we must remember what children really are—as opposed to our ideas of what they should be. While it may take some children fifteen seconds to make social contact with another child, it may take the quiet child at least fifteen minutes to make the same contact. We must be careful not to give undue

attention to what we choose to call "shyness." We cannot socialize for the child. We can establish an environment that guarantees that a child will have time for appropriate social action and avoid prodding our own children or others toward activities or interchanges they are not ready for—remembering that it takes a long time to learn to act within the conformity of social rules.

Do empower yourself.

Too often, when things are not going well, we place blame rather than accepting responsibility. I know, often at the cost of my own comfort, that I am the person who has the power to inspire, educate, and effect positive change in my school. I tell my parents that I would do anything for them except something that is wrong for their children—and not to expect that of me.

Teachers in my workshops often say, for example, "You don't understand. I can't change the system. I'm in a public school."

Private school teachers say, "The parents of our children have certain standards that prevent our doing things in certain ways."

It is the obligation of all human beings to do what is right for children. When, as adults, we know what is right, we must do what we can to make the system better. We must never waver from that ideal. Changes take time. Trying one new idea, changing one thing at a time, we will eventually make an impact.

Don't dwell in the past.

Respecting the uniqueness of each child and establishing an environment that pays attention to that uniqueness has always been a primary concern for me. At the same time, I have encouraged children to interact with other children. When I wrote *Before the Basics*, one of the rules I established for judging any activity for young children was to ask whether the activity is cooperative, whether it encourages children to think about others. Looking back, I now realize that I was not nearly so effective with questions of coaching as I could have been. I am not now focusing on what I failed to do then, but on becoming more effective for my students right now. All of us wish we could relive situations with new knowledge. Do not dwell in the past. Make a commitment now to openness and to change.

Make a commitment now to openness and to change.

Do question everything you do.

Ask yourself at the end of each day, "What have I learned today that could improve this program?" and ask of each experience you have presented or made possible for children, "Could I change this activity to open it up to more than one child?"

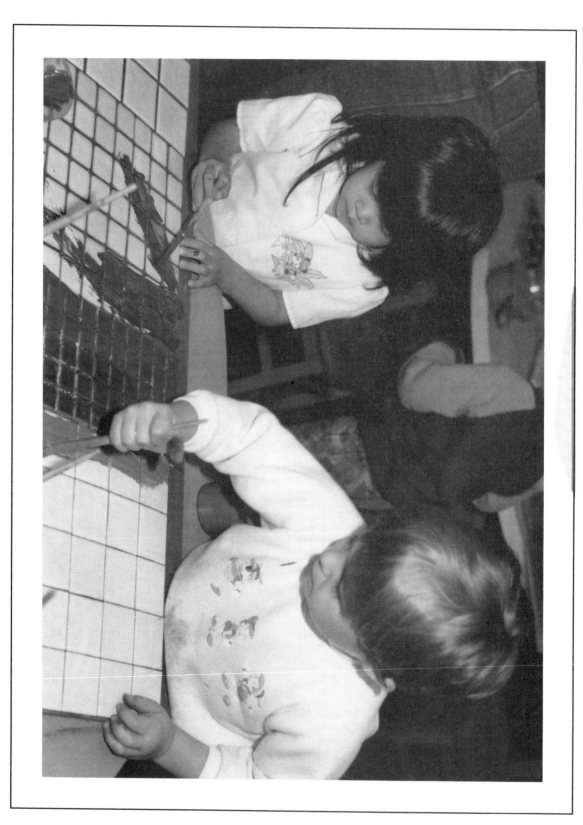

A

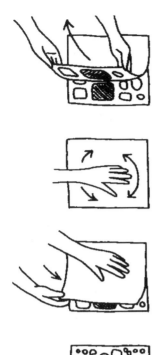

acting

nursery rhymes
stories and books
children's own creations
children as casting directors
acting during adult reading
animal sound tracks

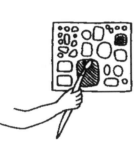

art

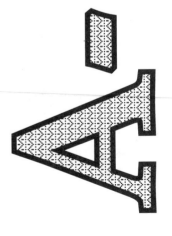

mural painting
tile painting
wallpaper collage
wallboard painting

acting out stories and books

Acting out stories and books encourages children to socialize without the pressure of being encouraged to "play with one another." Even the youngest child can be involved in this fine opportunity for coaction. I start with nursery rhymes. There are almost always ways to involve many children at a time. In "Jack and Jill," for example, four children can go up the hill together, or it's certainly possible to multiply "Little Miss Muffet" and the spider. The story line of almost any book can be acted out. An excellent book for this purpose is Pierr Morgan's *The Turnip* (New York: Philomel Books, 1990). Whether you are using nursery rhymes, songs, or books, props are not necessary, but a few are nice. Part of the spirit of this activity comes from the "audience" cheering the actors on.

- The ultimate stories to act out are, of course, stories the children have written themselves.

- Another option is to let the child who has written the story pick the other children to act the roles.

- Think about reading the story and while you are reading, letting all the children do the action words.

- If there are animals in the story, have the children make the animal sounds.

art

Art is essential to the young child. It is self-esteeming because it speaks to the uniqueness of each child, giving the child opportunities for expression and for power. It can take on many forms: art is basic science, basic math, language. It can be done inside—outside—with paint—with mud and sand. Expand your art to include possibilities for coaction.

Most often we think of art as being an individualized activity. We can, however, expand individual projects to include other children and thus opportunities for coaction. I am going to give you only a few examples here; there are others throughout this alphabet of coactivity. Your question with every art project should be "Could we expand this to include other children?"

- We have put clips for easel painting on a long, solid back fence. Occasionally we hang just one long piece of paper so as to encourage coactive mural painting.

- Attach a four-by-eight piece of wallboard to a wall. Depending on the number of children involved, you might want to use two or three sheets, if you have enough room. There are now several ways to proceed. Try one of the following techniques.

- We have used buckets of plaster (the mixture actually used by

- We have used buckets of plaster (the mixture actually used by sheetrock hangers), which the kids can slather on with plastic putty knives and other utensils. Then, because it doesn't dry quickly, they have time to poke bits and pieces of junk into it.

- Often, we paint it. We have four classes, and one class just paints over the top of the previous work.

- Wallboard can also be used for a collage of wallpaper. If you peel a big piece of contact paper and attach it to either a wall or a piece of wallboard, children can stick a wide variety of items onto it—feathers, paper, cotton balls, leaves, glitter.

- Tile painting is another way to get one child next to another. If one child starts painting from one side and another from the other side, what happens when they get to the middle? It is important that we stand back and simply listen to their negotiations, not solve the problem for them:

"I'm painting."
"I'm painting too."
"Oh, well, I guess I'll stop."
"Me, too."
"It's OK. I'll wait."

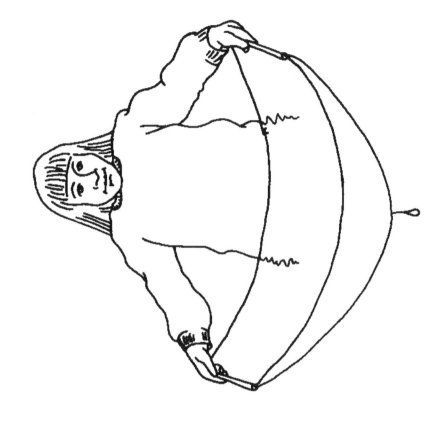

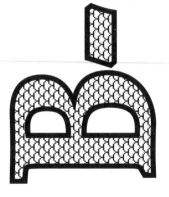

blocks

boxtop ball

bubbles

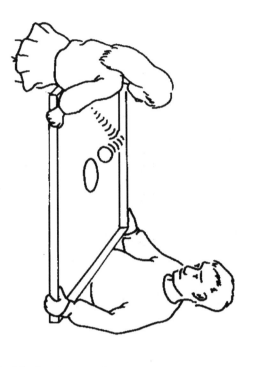

blocks

As with easels, blocks tend to disappear from the classroom and from homes after kindergarten. I think blocks are important long beyond that age frame. There is no such thing as having too many blocks. We have big plastic blocks, a large set of traditional wooden blocks, and small, multicolored blocks. Although I observe many children playing by themselves in the block area, I more often observe children working together at building with blocks.

- Realize that blocks encourage cooperative activity because they beg to be moved from one part of the room to the other. It's pretty hard to move some of those blocks by yourself (see "Moving Stuff").

- An extra set of blocks should be available for building outside, especially in the sand.

boxtop ball

While balls of all kinds encourage coactive play, and we use a wide variety of balls—old socks tied in knots, balls of newspaper, beach balls, Nerf® balls—one of the most successful toys we have constructed is delightful, inexpensive, and demands that two children play.

Made to be played with tennis balls, it's a rectangle, of wood, plastic, or cardboard, about eighteen by twenty-four inches with a two-inch

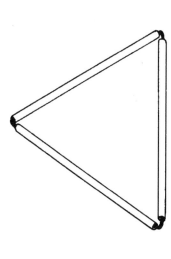

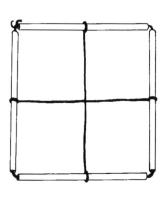

Bubble recipe: About a gallon of water and a half cup of Dawn liquid dish detergent. (I'm sorry to offer a commercial recommendation, but I've tried them all, and nothing works better than Dawn.) If you don't get magnificent bubbles, add just a little more Dawn.

You can buy fancy, expensive things to make bubbles, but I use straws and strings and hangers. I use plastic pop holders. I even use my hands.

edge. It could be made smaller. It has a shape cut out of the middle just big enough for a tennis ball to fall through. One child holds one end, another child the other. Often a third child sits on the floor, waiting to catch the dropping ball. The players rotate the box top—that is what it really looks like—a box top with a hole in the middle—and try to maneuver the ball into the hole. Sometimes they try to keep the ball from falling into the hole.

bubbles

We do bubbles often at our school. When I demonstrate the art of bubble making, I hear people saying they will do bubbles on the first "nice day," a special day, or the last day of school. Don't wait for a special occasion! We do bubbles every day.

Of course, the activity is ideal on damp days. Why? Because moisture in the air will make successful bubble making easier.

Bubbles really take at least two children—one to blow and one to run and catch. In addition, there are all those possibilities for just watching. At our school, there are always at least five or six children involved.

cardboard boxes

ceiling painting

cardboard boxes

Cardboard boxes of all shapes and sizes are good starters for coaction. Children can tape them together and paint them, and the boxes become houses, not ordinarily things a child would think of building without the help of other children. They can cut holes for windows, and the boxes will become not only houses, but hospitals, fire trucks, whole communities.

Many boxes taped together and painted often become dragons or "boxasaurs."

ceiling painting

Up in our loft, the ceiling is low enough so that if I staple a large piece of paper up, the children can paint on the ceiling. Painting on the ceiling by one child certainly always attracts five or six other children. Often I just sit on the stairs and listen to their conversations. They talk endlessly about how they could paint their bedrooms, and when they cannot quite reach, they discuss alternatives.

Sarah could not reach the high section of the ceiling. Suggestions came from the others:

"Stand on your tippy toes."
"Go get the high-heeled dress-up shoes."
"I'll bring you a chair."

None of the suggestions came from me because they didn't ask. Finally, after much discussion, another child lifted Sarah up.

She painted three strokes and left.

- If you do not have a loft or a ceiling low enough to allow for this activity, the "ceiling" of a large cardboard box works very well and demands even more coacting because the children are closer to each other.

- Tables also have "ceilings." We tape a piece of paper under the table, and children use felt pens or paint to create in the style of Michelangelo.

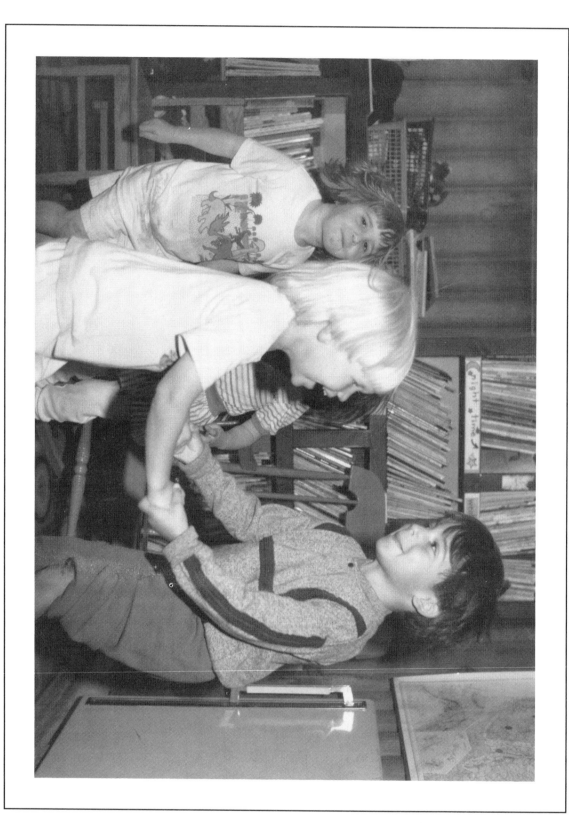

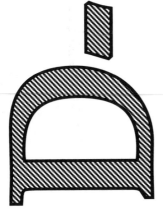

dancing

dressing up

dancing

Of course. But what kind? One of the most delightful songs I know for young children is "Waltzing with Bears." And waltzing is such a lovely movement for children. They don't have to count one, two, three, but just sway back and forth.

- Often I encourage small circles of children to waltz and sway to the music. While they can simply dance along, it is so much more fun for them to move with someone else. Especially fun is the kind of spontaneous dance that emerges when children are being sung to and have been asked for a suggestion for the next verse: Someone will respond, "Dance."

My question is always, "By yourself? Or with a partner?"

"With a partner. With two partners." And off we go!

dressing up

In our school, we allow children to wear dress-up outside, inside, and to paint in. Dressing up is not an activity children seem inclined to do alone, and often the dressing up game involves imitation of an adult activity—a wedding, a party, some family life situation. We all know how important it is that children be allowed to assume different roles and to practice for real life by expressing extremes in behavior without reprisal. Dressing up seems to be one of the most productive ways to encourage this role playing.

Dressing up has been removed from many classrooms because of adult obsessions with cleanliness or our fear of lice. Of course we are all concerned about cleanliness, but we need to control our concerns so as not to eliminate good experiences for children.

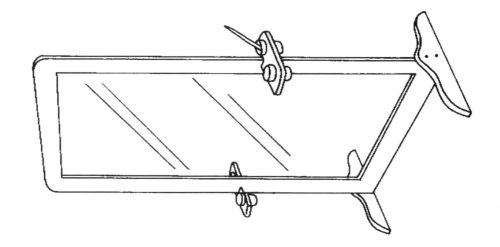

earth

engineering
construction
mud

easels

fence easels
plexiglass easels
wall easels

earth: engineering, construction, mud

Earth—wet earth, dry earth, mounds of earth, earth with holes dug into it! As I observe our children digging and piling and raking and shoveling, I think about how this environment allows and even encourages them to join together to accomplish their important tasks. Our children become incredibly good engineers as they build dams and tributaries, ponds and bridges across the ditches they dig.

I have a deep concern for children who are not allowed to make mud pies, who have no opportunity or who are not allowed to play in the dirt. We have to get back to letting children muck around in their own backyards.

If you've forgotten about the joy of making mudpies, read *Mud Pies and Other Recipes* by Marjorie Winslow.

I have often said, "I spent the first years of my life digging to China and didn't figure out until I was grown that someone filled in the holes at night so we could dig some more the next day."

It's a story you have heard often from many people. As a child, I was part of a large and poor family. After my mother took care of our needs, she sent us outside, and very often she locked the door. She said, "Play". She did not say with what, and we didn't have any toys. We had boards, a few nails, cans, and junk. We played games most of the time, fought, and dug holes in the backyard.

My mother was there if we needed her, but she didn't play referee. She didn't direct our play. She didn't hover. I can remember, though, on warm summer nights, my mother and father playing "Hide and Seek" with us and how wonderful it was and how I hated to go in. But they were rarely that obvious in their presence. We never saw them filling in the holes so we could dig them out again the next day.

easels

Easels need to be in all classrooms—preschool through eighth grade, at least. We have several different easels in our school. Painting at the easel is an option every day for our children.

- We have easels which are attached to the wall, where they cannot be kicked over or tripped over. Four children can paint at once, a situation that calls for much interaction and socializing while painting.

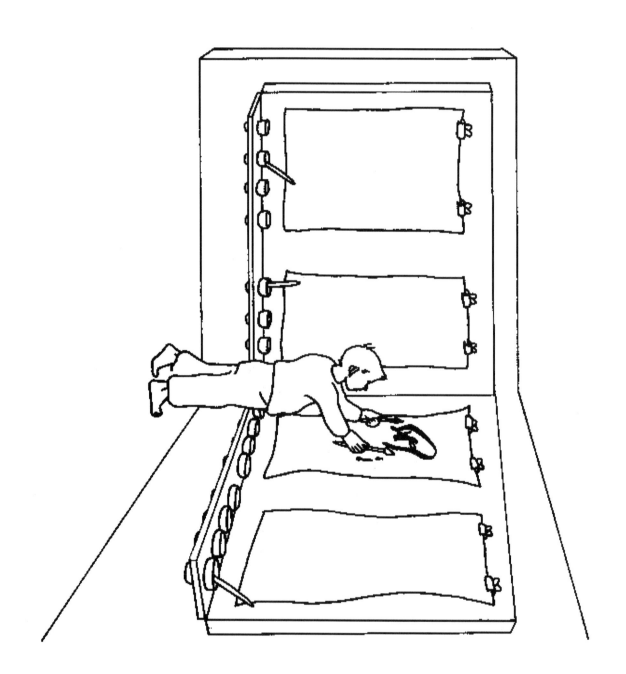

- We also have recently added easels to the back fence, where there is more freedom to spray or splatter paint.

- One of the most successful things we've ever done is to develop a plexiglass easel. It's two feet wide by four feet tall, and one child stands on one side and one on the other. They can see each other as they paint. Sometimes they peek around the edge of the easel; sometimes they make faces at each other. Often, I watch them communicate non-verbally.

- We have expanded this idea by making a triple easel, where six children can paint at once.

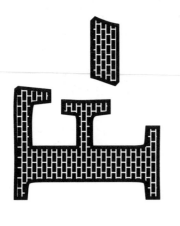

fingerplays

round and round the garden
here's a bunny with ears so funny
here's a bunny, sitting in the sun
keep off the grass
one potato, two potato

fingerpainting
flashlights
forts

fingerplays

All fingerplay lends itself to good coaction. Usually fingerplays are shown by the adult and the child copies the action. To promote coacting, try as often as possible to do fingerplays cooperatively. The fingerplays I love the most are the ones my mother taught me fifty years ago. Here are a few of my old standards.

- **Round and Round the Garden**

  "Round and round the garden" (First person: put hand out, palm up),

  "Like a teddy bear" (Second person: place index finger on first person's hand, going round and round the palm);

  "One step, two steps" (Second person: step index finger up first person's arm),

  "And tickle you under there" (Second person: tickle gently under first person's arm).

  Now, switch roles.

- **Here's a Bunny, Sitting in the Sun**

  "Here's a bunny, sitting in the sun" (First person: use the index and middle fingers of one hand to make the ears);

  "Along comes a little dog" (Second person: tap two fingers alternately to represent the dog chasing the bunny).

  "Watch that bunny run!" (First person: add directions).

- ### Here's a Bunny with Ears So Funny

  "Here's a bunny with ears so funny" (Put one hand up with index and middle fingers up, like rabbit ears),

  "And here's a hole in the ground" (With the other hand, make a circle with the index finger and thumb);

  "When a noise he hears, he picks up his ears" (Slightly lower and then raise index and middle fingers to make ears jump up)

  "And jumps in the hole in the ground" (Make the ears jump in by putting the index and middle fingers into the circle you've made with the other hand).

  Now everyone needs to get a partner and negotiate who's going to be the bunny and who will be the ears. Instead of fingers, the ears can be arms, and the rabbit hole can be made by forming a circle with your arms. You can further expand this to include two or three children making the hole and one or more children being the bunnies.

- **Keep Off the Grass**

This is the favorite fingerplay at our school.

On one person's palm, point out the city: "This is a house. This is a grocery store. This is the school. This is the street. And here's a park. In the park there are swings and slides and grass and flowers. And right over here there's a sign that says, "Keep off the grass!"

Then say, "Where's the grass?"

When the child points it out, gently slap the pointing hand and say, "Keep off the grass!!"

- **One Potato, Two Potato**

We start doing this in the traditional, individual way. Then we expand it. I ask the children for suggestions about how we could expand it. They do it on their heads, their tongues, on another person's back. We attempt all suggestions. The next step is to choose partners. One person puts a fist out first, and the next person puts a fist on top, and then the next and next, pulling the bottom hand out to add to the top, going as high as they can. This is difficult for young children, so however they do it is fine.

fingerpainting

When we fingerpaint, we do it directly on top of the table and take a print of the design when the child is ready. We do it this way for more than one reason. First of all, fingerpainting paper is expensive, and the quality is often poor. More important, children painting with their hands directly next to others' encourages conversation and problem-solving as colors become mixed.

flashlights

Buy the inexpensive kind and give two or three children flashlights. Have all the children turn the flashlights on and follow each other's beams.

- For a variation, place colored plastic or cellophane over the lenses of the flashlights.

forts

Whether they are permanent structures made of wood, improvisations made of stacked newspapers, or paper bags stuffed with newspaper and sealed with tape, forts provide an ideal play space (See "Moving Stuff").

games

going to kentucky
london bridge
down in the valley, two by two
detective

gutters

Going to Kentucky

Traditional

While go·ing to Ken·tuck·y, while go·ing to the fair, I

met a se·ño·ri·ta with flow·ers in her hair, so

shake it, ba·by, shake it, shake it if you can,

shake it like a milk·shake, and do the best you can, so

rum·ble to the bot·tom, rum·ble to the top,

turn 'n turn 'n turn 'n turn un·til you make a stop.

games

When planning any game, I think about how I can make it better for children and how I can promote coaction. Especially in the case of the young child, we can't get caught up in strict rules.

Think of the games we all played as children ourselves and how we made the rules up as we went along. I am very concerned about the emphasis placed these days on organized sports with strict rules. In my school, I try to emphasize games that are non-competitive, self-esteeming, and coactive. When I start a game that normally requires one child in the middle of a circle, for example, I immediately put two children into the middle. This helps decrease a child's anxiety over being the center of attention.

The definition of games is fun. The thesaurus lists these alternate words for fun—funmaking, good time, lovely time, pleasant time, big time or high time, time of one's life. Other synonyms for fun—rollick, gambol, celebration. In our world today there seems to be too little place for just fun.

• Going to Kentucky

For this game, put two children into the middle of a circle, while the rest stand in a larger circle around them. After the first run-through of the song, have those two choose where they are going, who will be the object of the meeting, and what's going to be in their hair. Sing the song again with their choices: "Going home with buttons in my hair," "Going to the grocery store with bananas in my hair," "Going to Disneyland with Donald Duck in my hair."

Everyone claps hands and dances in place. We smile and wave to the children in the middle. The two children in the middle shake their hands, heads, or whole bodies, whatever they like. Everybody sways and shakes to the ground and shakes back up. The two in the middle go around and around, pointing, until we shout, "Stop!" The children pointed at on "stop" are the next senoritas.

While going to Kentucky, while going to the fair,
I met a senorita with flowers in her hair.
Shake it baby, shake it! Shake it all you can!
Shake it like a milkshake, and do the best you can!
Now rumble to the bottom; now rumble to the top!
Turn and turn and turn, until you make a stop!

Variation: When the children turn, they pick two others to go to the center. Sometimes, rather than leaving the circle, the original choices remain so there are four in the middle, and we proceed until everyone is in the middle.

- **London Bridge**

Some of the best fun we have in our school is taking an old game and changing the rules to make it fit the play of young children. One wonderful example is "London Bridge." If you have only one bridge, young children will lose interest before it is their turn to go through, or they will get impatient and start pushing. We shout, "We need lots of bridges!" Sometimes we seem to have more bridges than children going through, but that's the fun of playing games with young children: they love to help solve this kind of problem.

- ## Down in the Valley, Two by Two

We are very relaxed about how we play games. With this game, we encourage the children to find partners; often they do this game in groups of three. While singing the song, they weave back and forth, going from a standing position to a squatting position until we sing, "Rise, Sally, rise!" Then the children negotiate—one of them is leading and makes a motion, and the other child or children follow. Next, it is the other child's turn to choose the motion that partners will do. We also play this as a circle game with one or two children in the middle making a motion and then picking another child to go into the center.

I teach this delightful game and song to adults in workshops, and often the most remarkable thing happens. Having been given the directions for the game, participants are able to find partners and can manage to weave together and go to the floor, but when I sing, "Make a motion, two by two," surprisingly large numbers of adults simply imitate my motion, having, I presume, no confidence in their ability to initiate a motion of their own.

I offer this comment not to criticize, but as a reminder that we need to care for the child inside us and be able to develop our own confidence and social skills before we can help children develop the social skills we believe they should have.

Down in the Valley, Two by Two

Traditional

● **detective**

The secret to having fun with this game, a variation of "Policeman, Policeman" as presented in *Before the Basics* (91-93) , is not taking it too seriously.

Choose an object to be hidden. We often use a small stuffed animal. One child sits in a chair or on the floor, eyes closed; don't take this part too seriously and insist on a blindfold. The object is placed   behind the child and then quickly taken by another child chosen by the teacher, parent, or another child. The second child hides the object.

The child that is "it" now opens his or her eyes and I begin to ask questions of the group to help the child find the object. What color hair does the child who took the toy have? What color pants? What color eyes? Is it a boy or girl?

This game develops an awareness of others for young children. Often, they will say with such surprise, "Oh, she has the same color hair as me!"

Once a child said, "I didn't even know you were here today!"

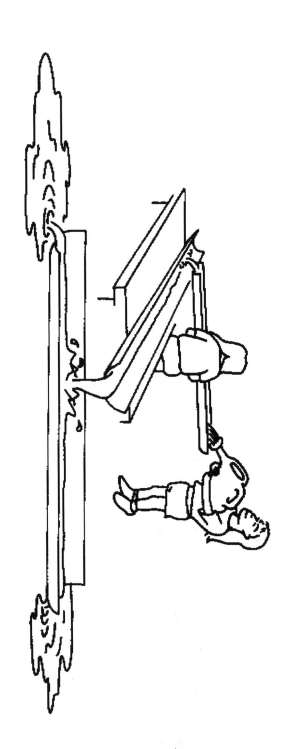

gutters

Plastic gutters cut into many different lengths—some with holes drilled in them—almost automatically require two children to handle. They can be used for great water play. They can also be used between two chairs to run cars back and forth or at an angle for car or ball races. I'm certain if you leave some out for your children they will find all sorts of other possibilities.

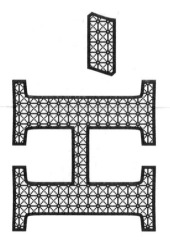

hand-me-downs

"hello" in many languages

hide and go seek

hand-me-downs

We have baskets and baskets of hand-me-down clothing at our school—different from dress-up clothing—for children who need a change while at school. Sometimes they get wet deliberately just so they can go pick out a "new" outfit. At other times, they simply say they need different clothes and proceed to change. While these are old clothes, they are always new to the children. This is their opportunity to choose their own outrageous outfits without the interference of adult opinion. It is also a natural opportunity for coaching. I seldom see a child changing without asking the advice of another child: "How do you think I look?" "Does this fit me?"

"hello" in many languages

One of the things we want children to know is that we all live on this planet with many other people. It's a concept that takes time to develop. Saying "hello" is one of the first things our children learn. Saying it in other languages seems an appropriate place to start developing a global perspective.

Chinese: Ni hao (knee/how)
French: Bon jour (Bone/zhoor)

Italian: Bon giorno (Bone/jor/know)
Japanese: Konnichi wa (con/knee/chee/wah)
Regional American dialects: Howdy, How de do, Hi, y'all
Spanish: Ola (Oh/la)
Swahili (East Africa): Jambo (Jam/bo)

hide and go seek

Forget the traditional rules. With preschoolers, when you say, "Hide,"
they will all hide in the same place and for only thirty seconds. It's
more like "Hide and Chase and Laugh," but obviously a wonderful
opportunity for coacting.

ice

ice cube painting

ice castles

ice

Place blocks of ice, big or small according to your own choice, into a tub or a clean kitty litter pan. You can even put the ice outside on the cement. Have the children pour small amounts of food coloring over the blocks; as a variation, they can use eyedroppers to drop the color onto the blocks.

The colors mix. Outside, the sun shines on the project and adds another dimension to looking through the block. If you're doing this on a cloudy day, you might use a flashlight with the project.

Next, add salt (regular or rock salt) to get holes in the ice. Having children next to each other, experiencing the excitement of this "event" together, encourages coactivity. A word of caution: An adult should be present when you bring out the salt, since it is dangerous for young children to eat salt in quantity.

- Igloos are also a possibility if you have lots of small ice cubes. You can stick them together by using salt, and food coloring can be dripped on these, too. It takes a lot of salt to make the ice cubes stick together, though.

ice cube painting

If you freeze colored water in ice cube trays, children can paint with the ice cubes. You can put a popsicle stick in each section to provide a little more control for the child, but I like their hands to be wet, cold, and a different color. If you have plain ice cubes, they can be dipped in food coloring or tempera paint.

In order to get bright colors, use two ounces of food coloring to two cups of cubes. I use only primary colors—red, blue, yellow. The others come naturally. The paper needs to be varied—large, small, varying in shape, slick, absorbent. Even coffee filters will work nicely here.

ice castles

The day before we do ice castles, I freeze water in every imaginable container at school. On the way to school, I stop at the local grocery store and buy five or six big blocks of ice.

You can do this project inside or outside. Inside, it's best to put the ice forms in clean kitty-litter pans. Outside, we put the big blocks of ice on a large wooden table. We provide small cups of regular salt and slightly diluted food coloring with eye droppers, which the children abandon for the cups about two seconds into the project. The children pour salt all over the big blocks and start building by attaching the various ice shapes. We do this for a couple of weeks because the children demand it. The morning classes always ask, "Did the afternoon class take it home?"

Dear Parents:

We need your help. For the next few weeks, we will be building ice castles. Please freeze water in every imaginable container—paper cups, gelatin molds, cone-shaped cups, cake pans, icebox dishes, small buckets. Please send twenty pieces of ice as often as you can.

Love,

Teacher Bev.

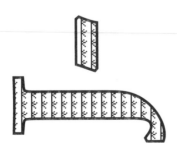

journals

jumping

journals

Even the journal, normally a highly private activity, can provide opportunities for coaching. All children in our school have journals in the form of spiral bound notebooks. I explain to them at the beginning of the year that what goes into these books is anything so important that they don't want to forget it. Journals are put out on a small table every day. I remind the children that the journals are out for them if they need to add anything today. Our children do not do the writing in these books, although they could if they wished. Instead, they dictate to an adult. When I am aware of important events in their lives, I will suggest that they go into the journals, but not pressure children to write them up.

These journals are private and are not read aloud to the class. They are kept at school and do not go home until the end of the year. The value of journals in connection with coactivity is that children can recognize in them their own social progress.

Jimmy ran in from outside one day and said, "Get my journal. Open it up. Write down 'Today.' Write 'I hate Trevor.'"

Then he said, "Read it to me," and then said, "That's all."

About two weeks later, he came back, asked for the journal again and asked me to read where he had said he hated Trevor. Then he said, "Now. Write down 'Today.' Now write 'I like Trevor.'"

jumping

When I encourage children to change an action in a song, they often suggest jumping. My immediate response is always, "Alone or with a friend?" Often they ask to do it with a friend. Then I ask, "With your eyes closed or open?"

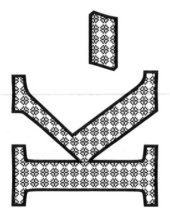

kindergarten

knock-knock jokes

kindergarten

During our parent orientation this September, at which we covered all aspects of our school, including child development, appropriate environments for children and adult participation, I asked if there were any questions.

One parent quietly asked, "What happens when my child leaves this environment? What do I do about kindergarten? What do I do about first grade?"

I am often asked these questions in different ways. Often, teachers will ask during workshops, "How do the children do when they leave your school?"

My answer is always the same: we cannot prepare children for the next life. We must provide an environment that is appropriate for the child's stage of development.

It is the obligation of all parents and teachers--everyone who cares about education--to demand appropriate environments for children. I know thousands of caring, hard-working tezchers who are crying for parent involvement. I know many parents who would help, if they knew what to do. We are all in this together.

knock-knock jokes

Young children don't have highly developed senses of humor. For some reason, though, they love knock-knock jokes. Even though they may not understand them or create ones that make any sense, it is the laughing together that is valuable.

"Knock, knock."
"Who's there?"
"Lettuce."
"Lettuce who?"
"Lettuce in and you'll find out."

This was my granddaughter's favorite joke when she was two. She got it a bit mixed up and would say, "Salad in and you'll find out."

"Knock, knock."
"Who's there?"
"Duane."
"Duane who?"
"Duane the bathtub. I'm dwowning."

And yet another:

"Knock, knock."
"Who's there?"
"Boo."
"Boo who?"
"Don't cry. It's only a joke."

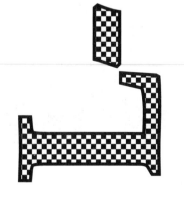

ladders

laundry

lofts

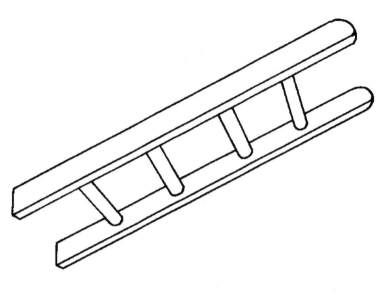

ladders

One of the fathers in our school made ten ladders for our children. They are short enough for safety and small enough for one child to carry, although usually two children work together with them. I wish you could observe all the activities our children do with these ladders. Conventionally, of course, they put them against sturdy wooden boxes and climb up to the top. But, just as often, they lay them flat on the ground, and three or four children sit between the rungs and pretend they are in a boat. They place them against a small mound of dirt and pretend they are mountain climbers.

The father that made them came back a few weeks after he had delivered them to see how we were doing. He couldn't believe what he saw: "They look ten years old!" And he was right. In a month, they had been so loved and used, they looked as if they already needed to be replaced.

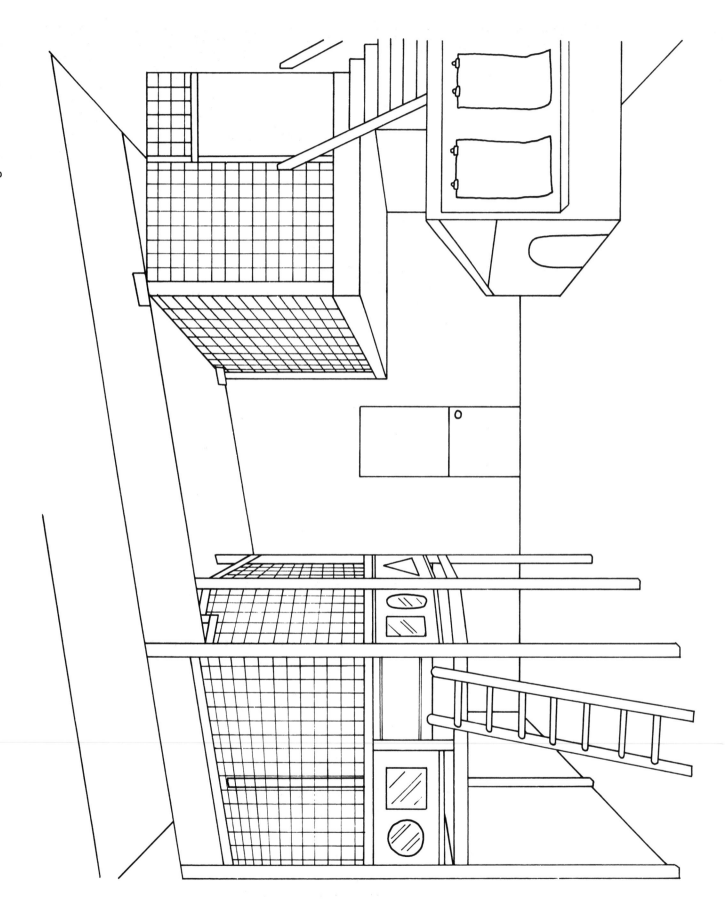

laundry

Our ancestors used to walk to the river, pound their clothes against the rocks, and socialize. In a later generation, we hung clothes on the line and talk with our neighbors as we did. Socializing then was often attached to the necessities of life.

In this day of automatic washing machines, the opportunities for socialization have lessened. In our school, we have an old washtub and a washboard and wooden clothes bars. One of our children's favorite outdoor activities is washing clothes. I'll assure you that most of our children had no idea what the clothes racks were for. They didn't know how to wring the water from the clothes until I showed them how two children working together could twist a piece of clothing. They also did a lot of problem solving together, deciding how various sizes of clothing needed to be placed on the racks in order to fit.

lofts

If you are fortunate enough to be in on the initial planning of a school or your own child's bedroom, be sure to include a loft or platform where children can get up and away from the rest of the world. Lofts can be easily added to already-existing structures and can, in fact, double your space.

We have two lofts in our school. They weren't there when we started. In one we have the playhouse equipment. It is enclosed by a smooth wire for safety (see the entry on weaving, page 155, for how we expand and use this necessity to our advantage). In the other loft, the walls are mounted with Duplo® boards with baskets of Duplo® blocks close by. Part of the remaining walls have sections of plexiglass which are used for a variety of activities. Our children draw on them with water-based pens or push vinyl shapes onto them. On some, we have glued seashells. For us the possibilities are endless. I have no doubt that next month, we will change or add something to the loft.

Recently, we cut a hole in the floor and added a plexiglass section. I wish you could see the coacting as children below discover the children in the loft above—and vice-versa. Generally, adults do not go up to the lofts. It is a place for children to laugh and to be together away from hovering adults.

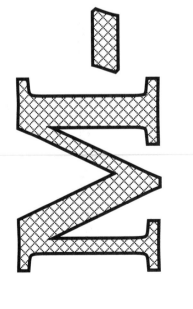

M

milk

mixing ages

moving stuff

mud

milk

We do a science experiment at our school that draws a huge crowd of participants and more socializing and conversation than almost anything else we do.

Into a pie pan, pour two cups of warm milk (not hot). If you are unwilling to "waste food," you could use milk from the school cafeteria that would otherwise be dumped out. You could also discuss the problem of wasting food with children.

Drop at least six drops of food coloring onto the milk (I use the three primary colors). Then drip in a few drops of liquid dish detergent and stand back. The milk will churn and move. The colors will blend and make new colors.

Children automatically talk to one another while watching this experiment. The explanation to offer your children is that the detergent emulsifies the fats in the milk and causes the movement. My children love to say the word "emulsify."

- You could start with yellow and blue and get green or red and yellow to get orange.

- Try the experiment with nonfat milk and compare the results with what you get from regular milk.

- Try the experiment without warming the milk and see what happens.

mixing ages

The ages of the children in our school range from two years and nine months to five years (occasionally six). Older children help younger children with all sorts of things—helping them dress, pulling them in wagons, teaching them how to pump on the swing, how to pedal a tricycle. When we have only three- or four-year-olds in a classroom, we tend to be more restrictive in our curriculum, and perhaps inappropriately so. We have always been advocates of mixing ages in our school, and I am delighted to see that NAEYC-published results of preliminary findings in this area (Lilian Katz et al., *The Case for Mixed-Age Grouping in Early Education* [Washington, D.C., 1990]) seem to suggest that our practice offers benefits.

No child is ever just three or four years old. Every child has some of the needs of a younger or older child. In a mixed-age setting, children are given the opportunity to re-experience the things they missed earlier or allowed the space to experiment with something meant for an older child.

For me, this is never-ending. There is great value, for example, in cross-age tutoring in elementary school, where older children can thus reinforce their knowledge by teaching it to younger children.

Younger children often have almost a sense of worship toward older children and sometimes will give greater credence to knowledge imparted from a child tutor. In families of only one or two children and in neighborhoods where whole families are gone the entire day, our children are missing the opportunity to experience being the older

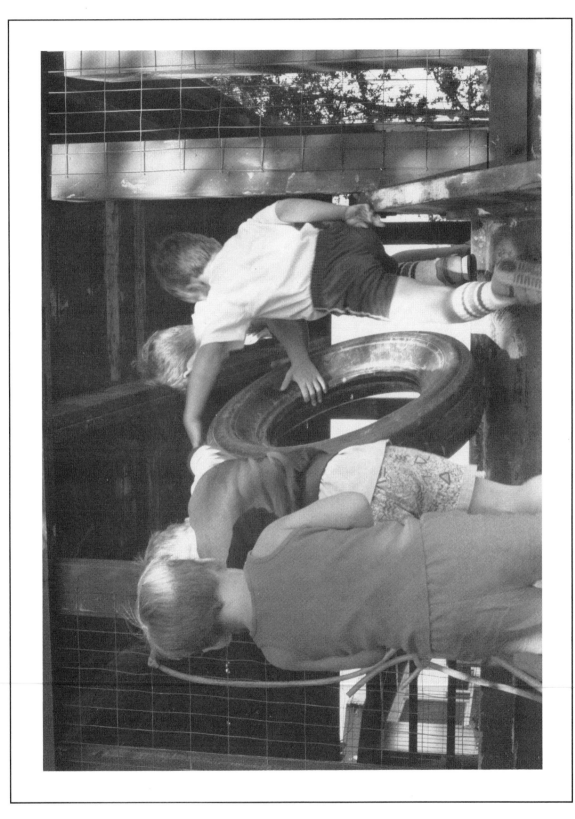

child or the youngest child. If we isolate them in school and day care centers as well by grouping them by age, will they miss out entirely on the experiences that mixing ages can bring?

moving stuff

One of the things I know is that children need to move "stuff" from one part of the room or house to another in order to see how it works in a different place. Another thing I'm just as certain of is that adults would much rather have things stay in the same place. That's why we can never find things when our children are little: they know they need to move it to understand it, and when they are through understanding, they immediately abandon it and move onto another important project and cannot be concerned with where that "stuff" is any more.

Blocks, for example, have to move. They have to be used in sand and dirt (use your older blocks, or buy two sets if you are concerned about their being dirty). We have eleven grandchildren, and every time they come over, they all head for the back yard. They drag out big pieces of wood (twelve inches long by six inches wide and an inch thick) and start building something new. They never use nails: they just stack and move. Then they get an old sheet and drape and tuck it around the wood. They never tire of this kind of play and rarely quarrel. I have heard, however, some heated discussions and observed some incredibly intense coactive work.

The first discussion is always about who is going to move the wood up to the patio. All of them, without exception, not counting the youngest

...nothing an adult builds will be quite as much fun as when children do it themselves.

grandchild, claim that they did it the last time. After a few minutes of negotiation, they always agree to do it together. Then the next thing they negotiate is how to move it. Very soon the question is how high the walls should be. What about food for the house? Then they start dividing the fort up into spaces for everyone. In time, I will be asked to come up with food and sheets to make it real, but nothing an adult builds will be quite as much fun as when children do it themselves.

mud

Our yard at school is sand and dirt. Every day our children add water to it and make the most wonderful mud. They dig, channel rivers, build bridges and roads, dam up the water, and have many creative conversations. In addition to learning about engineering, absorption, and conservation, they learn to work together on big projects.

It is an important part of childhood to mix and stir and dig. If you have a problem with the "mess" (personally, I have a policy never to use the word), have changes of clothing for those children who want to change. I see cleaning up as part of the process. Children need to be given real jobs to do, they have a real feeling of contribution and community. It is important for children to feel the pleasure of working productively toward a goal.

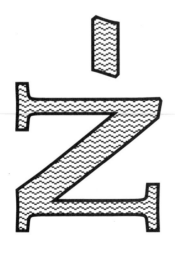

N

newspaper forts

newspaper sculpture

nurturing

newspaper forts

What you need is many Sunday papers, folded back into their original forms—in other words, neatly organized. Lay one paper flat and place the next paper next to it tightly. Continue this process for at least eight feet in one direction and five feet in another. As in laying brick, for the next layer, place each paper centered on the crack where the two papers below it meet. Continue until the structure is at least three feet tall. This takes an incredible amount of work and coaxing to get it straight. As in many projects, it's process that is more important than product here, but this is a product the children can paint or drape sheets over when it's done for a wonderful place to play.

newspaper sculpture

Begin by rolling newspapers, at least three rolls per child, preferably more. Tape the rolls and have the children shape the newspaper rolls as they choose. Have lots of masking tape ready and start attaching the rolls to one another. You can start by attaching to the floor, the ceiling, a piece of cardboard, or even the wall. The result will be a free-form sculpture of impressive magnitude. The class may add to the sculpture over a period of days or even weeks. It can be painted or decorated with sticky dots, string, ribbons, glue and glitter, or whatever the children imagine and suggest. The sculpture succeeds with a wide range of ages. One benefit of this project is that children are placed in a situation requiring negotiation and group planning with-a wide range of ages. One benefit of this project is that children are placed in a situation requiring negotiation and group planning without even realizing it.

- Suggestion: You will need help to roll enough newspaper rolls. Enlist parents. Older children can help with the rolling.

nurturing

Parents come to our school excited about their own children's opportunities to grow and have glorious fun in this new environment. In the beginning, parents stay very close to their own children. By the second or third week of school, though, usually during storytime, when other children are likely to climb onto their laps, they begin to become aware of children other than their own. They discover their laps will hold more than one child. One of the great advantages of having parents involved in our program is that they too learn about coactivity.

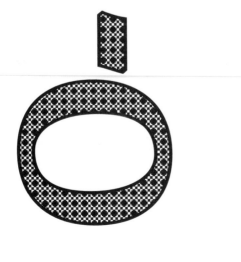

outside space

outside space

Children would rather be outside than inside even in the most inclement weather. Our children are free to choose to be outside the minute they arrive in the morning. How we set up an outside space for them in schools and homes is crucial to their development.

What we need outside for school is space, dirt, sand, water, trees, and a hard top area for riding tricycles. We need wagons and wheelbarrows and stuff for children to haul in them. We need water and funnels and plastic hoses for experimenting. We need cups with holes drilled in them so that the water will run out. We need space to do bubbles on a grand scale.

Children need space to run, a place to yell, a place where adults are not hovering and directing each activity. We have no qualms about taking outside everything we do inside.

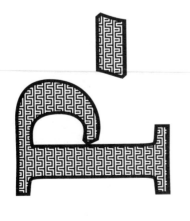

painting (large-scale)

plexiglass

puzzles

painting (large-scale)

Children at our school paint everything. Well, just about everything. Painting at easels and fingerpainting are just two of our painting activities. We also do it on a grander scale.

The parents at our school built a three-story fort. They stained it brown. The children were so disappointed that it was only a single color that we gave them large pans of tempera paint in all colors and they painted every part of the fort they could reach. Each class painted—even over the previous coats.

We would allow them to paint every day if they wanted to. The school really belongs to them. I do make clear to them what I don't want them to paint—like my car out in front of the school. Given the space, the trust, the time, and the paint, this project can develop not only coaching skills but a sense of excitement, power, and uniqueness. Because we emphasize the process instead of the product, the project gives a tremendous sense of belonging to a community.

plexiglass

Children socialize nonverbally long before verbal communication is fully developed. We have put pieces of plexiglass everywhere imaginable in our school.

We have put plexiglass on the floor of a loft, where children can look up and see those in the loft and vice versa. A four-year-old at our school put together a large puzzle upside down on the plexiglass in the loft. He put it together by shape only, not by the picture. When he was through, he ran and got several friends and proudly showed them the puzzle from below.

Anywhere there is a wall, cut out a space and insert plexiglass. Children can draw on it, stick on and maneuver pieces of vinyl, press their faces up against it to communicate with children on the other side. We have made a plexiglass table so that when children finger-paint, other children can watch from underneath.

I can't emphasize how creative you need to be about this. Often I will observe a brief, non-verbal encounter between two children on either side of a piece of plexiglass. Sometimes that's all it is. At other times, it can be the catalyst for an extended period of play. The barrier of plexiglass seems to give a sense of protection that allows for a feeling of power. Children can make faces and be silly, expressing a wide variety of feelings, with less risk of physical encounter.

puzzles

Puzzles are often thought of as being an individual activity. They are even better when two or more children do them together. We have a wide variety of skill levels and sizes in our puzzles. We do them on the floor, under tables, up in lofts, and even on the table top.

When a child needs help with a puzzle, I always suggest getting help from another child. Can you remember how it felt to get help from a friend? How the two of you communicated to solve the problem and how good it felt not to require an adult solve your problem for you?

Maximum coacting occurs when the puzzle has been made from a whole book the children are familiar with. You can't imagine the conversations that go on about which page comes first and what action took place on a particular page.

how to make puzzles

First, select a picture and get your tools and materials together. You will need a saw, a piece of Masonite™ or hardboard to fit the picture, rubber cement, wood, glue, scissors or razor blade, a paper cutter or ruler, clothespins, sandpaper, and a pencil.

Next, cut your picture to fit the piece of hardboard and use a paper cutter or ruler to even out the edges.

Now, coat the back of the picture and one side of the hardboard with rubber cement. Work carefully, since rubber cement bonds to itself. Cover the dry rubber cement on the hardboard with a piece of plain white paper, moving the paper so half an inch of the hardboard is exposed. Position the picture and press it down onto the exposed back. Now, slowly pull the plain white paper down so that the picture and hardboard bond together without bubbles.

Trim the picture with the razor blade, and using the saw, cut the frame for the puzzle. Draw a one-half-inch line from each edge and cut from the outer edge of the hardboard to the line, rounding the corners.

Cut the picture into jig-saw shaped pieces, avoiding creating pieces that might break when handled.

Spread wood glue where frame and puzzle touch. Press the frame and puzzle back together, placing clothespins around the outer edge of the puzzle. Remove the excess glue from around the frame and let dry.

After the puzzle has dried, you may cover it with clear contact paper or seal with a water-based shellac or high gloss spray. If necessary, you may sand the pieces for a smoother fit.

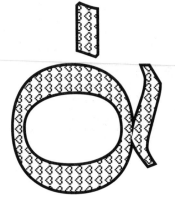

q

quiet places

quilting

quiet places

We need to provide quiet places throughout the school, in day care centers, and at home. There need to be places for small groups of children, two or three, to play quietly, to whisper, to giggle, to get away from the crowds. It's easier than you think. Blankets or sheets can be draped over tables, two chairs. Large pillows can be tucked into quiet corners. An old sheet can be tied between two posts outside to form a hammock.

quilting

During Pajama Week at our school, we have the children each bring a piece of material, six by six inches, from an old piece of clothing. These pieces can be laid down in the shape of a quilt. Each child shares the "history" of this piece of material—how it was a part of his or her life. In this way, our children gain an awareness of what place in a social community means as well as a better sense of themselves.

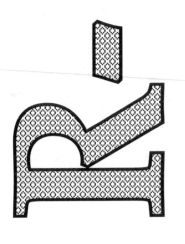

R

rainbow stew

reading

refrigerator doors

rainbow stew

A very successful project from *Mudpies to Magnets* is rainbow stew. Recipe for rainbow stew: Mix one-third cup sugar, one cup corn-starch, and four cups of cold water. Cook until thick and divide into three bowls. Add a generous amount of red, blue, and yellow food coloring to the bowls. You want the colors to be bright. Ask the child, "What colors do you want in your bag?" Then into a heavy-duty sealable bag, place about three tablespoons of each color they've requested. I roll the bag to push the air out and then seal and tape it closed with duct tape.

The children will knead, squish, and manipulate the balls of color into every possible color combination.

- Now we have expanded on this project at our school. Friends in Florida told me about this idea one Saturday, and the very next Monday, we tried it. Imagine, if you will, a very large plastic bag—the size of a bed—with gallons of rainbow stew in all colors. Find a plastic bag used to wrap a mattress or something as large. Take the recipe and multiply it by six. Mix two batches that size for each color. This will produce enough for a queen-size bag. The process is the same. We sealed the bag with duct tape. The children used their whole bodies to knead the stew. They lay on it, sat on it, crawled on it, walked barefoot on it, sometimes chanting, "Red and yellow and blue and green." The most interesting thing to me was that in the small bag, the colors mixed almost immediately. In the larger bag the colors stayed distinct much longer—more like a real rainbow.

reading

Story time provides wonderful opportunities for coacting, but don't forget all the coaction that can occur when a child is excited about a book and wants to share that excitement with a friend.

refrigerator doors

At our school instead of dedicating space to bulletin boards, we use the space for old refrigerator doors attached to the walls. They can be half doors or whole doors. We paint them bright colors. Then we attach magnets to the backs of a myriad of things. We especially like the wooden characters from Childwood.™ We also use things like sea shells, small cars and trucks, small blocks in different shapes, and pieces of leftover plexiglass. Leftovers from almost anything can be attached to magnets.

What I observe, over and over, is children using the magnets to tell each other stories. We are already planning to add a car door to our collection.

S

sand towers

snack

songs

spider swinging

stretchers

sand towers

Our whole yard consists of sand or dirt, a situation which makes it easy for us to dig and play, but even in a small sand pile, sand towers are great fun. When we do sand towers, it includes many children, and even the quietest child becomes an avid observer.

Encourage the children to push dry sand into a pyramid, as much as they can. With their thumbs, they are to push a small indentation in the top of the mountain of sand and then pour water from a small measuring cup into the indentation. The trick is to pour slowly, trying not to spill over the edge of the indentation. How much to pour? It takes practice. Perhaps three-quarters of a cup would be good for a small tower.

After pouring the water, they need to scoop away the dry sand carefully, and what is left is a wonderful tower. It looks like an airplane control tower to many children.

We build them all over the yard and then, because we can do it again, we knock them down and begin again. If you don't have a play yard full of sand, use a large tray with sand on it.

snack

As adults, we are very well- conditioned to the social opportunities that accompany food . Snack provides a multitude of ways for children to make positive social contact.

songs

When I think of ways to include children in the most positive way, I think of music. When I gather my children together with a stroke of my autoharp and we start singing, most of the children participate. Even children who never sing at school will often sing at home, and I can see from the expressions on their faces that they are enjoying the time together.

It is important to think "inclusion" when doing music with children. When I sing a song, my thought is always, "How can the children change the words, the action of this piece?"

I never pressure children to give an answer about changing songs, but I do encourage each child in a gentle way to give an individual answer. When they see that all answers are acceptable, many children will find the courage to share their answer. Even if their answer has been offered before, I never say, "Oh, we just did that. Can you think of another?"

What I do is try to set it up beforehand by saying, "Okay, Susan, we've clapped and danced and jumped. Can you think of another thing we could do?"

I always accept whatever answer is offered. When a child answers, "Jump!" I ask, "Do you want to jump by yourself or with a friend?" or sometimes add "How many friends?" Recently a child said, "I want to jump with three friends and do it with our eyes closed."

The advantage of music is that it incorporates every emotion. It gives children courage and ways to work through their concerns. I can never seem to find words adequate to express how passionately I believe in the positive effects music has in working with young children.

spider swinging

When a child is swinging, if another child sits on the first child's lap, facing, with legs hanging out the back of the swing, we call it spider swinging. It's a wonderful opportunity for children to laugh and talk to each other.

stretchers

It's very difficult to carry a stretcher all by yourself! For this encouragement to coaction, you'll need two wooden dowels, each an inch thick and about two or two and one-half feet long, and a piece of sailcloth about fourteen inches wide with a three-quarter-inch hem on both sides to form pockets for the dowels. We provide bandages, elastic bandages, and stethoscopes as well. Often our children can be seen running bandaged bears and dolls to a cardboard box hospital.

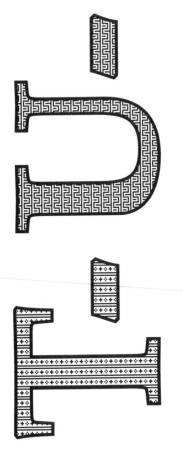

teddy bears
toilet paper
train tables
tricycles

umbrellas
underwear

teddy bears

We do this during Pajama Week, but the activity could be done any time, especially in connection with reading *The Teddy Bear's Picnic*.

Each child is encouraged to bring a teddy bear or any other stuffed animal to school—one that the child feels comfortable leaving overnight. If a child doesn't have one, I lend them one. Before leaving school, the children tuck their teddies into bed and tell them to have a good night, that they'll see them the next day.

Before the children come in the next morning, the teddy bears and I have a party. One of them sits on the toilet, and I put yellow food coloring in the bowl. Two or three are by the easels, paint brushes taped to their paws. A painting has been done on the easel. I knock chairs over and put bears on top of them and under them. I put scraps of food in different places with bears close by.

In the morning, I greet the children out in front of the school, making sure all of them are there before we open the door and go in. What I say is, "You will not believe what those bears did while you were gone!"

The most interesting thing is the way all the children pitch in to help clean up, saying things like, "Well, my bear did this, so I'd better help." They are much more serious about it than I ever expected them to be. What I love about the activity is the "we're all in this together" attitude.

toilet paper

We buy inexpensive toilet paper and offer a roll as each child arrives at school. Since we have twenty-four children at a time, that's twenty-four rolls, at least. We never give directions for its use.

I wish you could be there to see all the creative ideas and hear all the conversation and observe all the coactive play that goes on. They unravel the whole roll by themselves and make huge piles to jump or lie down in.

One child used his roll to fingerpaint with and then took it home and each day talked about how it unpeeled, layer by layer. Other children wrapped me up in it and stuffed it into my shirt and pants. They wrapped each other up like mummies and then burst out of the wrap.

We laughed until we cried. Nobody fought, nobody argued, and nobody flushed any of the paper down the toilet. At the end of each class session, we swept the paper into a pile and left it for the next day.

It is interesting to me that following the activity I left a couple of rolls out for weeks and no one played with them. They had played with toilet paper until they knew everything that could be done with it. I asked the children how long they thought they would remember playing with toilet paper. One child said he would remember it until he was a grandfather.

train table

We have a wooden train set. What makes it special is that the table for it has a hole cut in the center. Two or three children can get into the center and work while others work from the sides and ends. I have observed children at the train table, and it is rarely good friends who play at the table together: it is children who love the train, so we see a mix of ages and personalities. We also use this table for building with small blocks.

tricycles

As you might expect, the trikes I like the best are the ones that have a place in back for another child to ride or a place to haul all sorts of stuff.

umbrellas

As sweet as they are, our children can always play unsheltered in the rain without melting, but a nice thing to have on hand for them—in any weather—is an assortment of umbrellas. It is truly a lovely experience to observe two children, strolling in the rain, sharing an umbrella. Often you can purchase quite inexpensive larger umbrellas that can be planted in the ground for two children to sit under.

underwear

With all the water play we do, we have baskets of spare clothes. Usually, the adults do not have to help the kids find a suitable set of underwear. In fact, as the teacher, I discourage adult interference. Children are really good at helping each other find just the right color and size. When I listen behind the door, I hear, "Do you like this color? Is this your size?" (See Dressing Up)

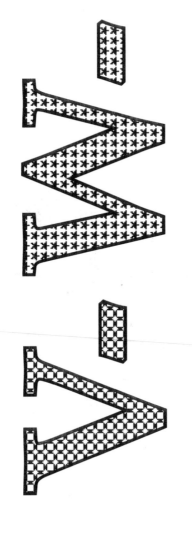

velcro®

volcanoes

wagons and wheelbarrows

washcloths, towels,
and hankies

water tables

weaving

velcro®

You can attach Velcro® to the edges of many things, walls included, and then attach the other side of the Velcro® to sheets. When children match these pieces up to the ones on the walls, they have tents. The possibilities for coaching are limitless.

volcanoes

A volcano can be done inside or outside. You will need a plastic pint bottle with a narrow neck that a cork will fit. Outside, bury the bottle up to its neck in sand. Inside the school, we bury the bottle in sand in a dishpan. Put into the buried bottle two or three teaspoons of baking soda, a few drops of detergent (if you want bubbles), and some red food coloring. Pour about a quarter to a third of a cup of vinegar down into the bottle. Quickly put the cork on the bottle. Stand back! When all participants wind up with red "lava" all over their faces and are reduced to tears from laughing, I know the volcano has helped develop a sense of belonging to a group.

wagons and wheelbarrows

These are two wonderfully coactive pieces of equipment necessary for all children.

washcloths, towels, and hankies

When was the last time you did something with your child that would establish or pass on a family tradition? A cost-free, but priceless way to pass down stories--true or make-believe--about yourself as a child or about your family is to tell stories with washcloths, towels, or hankies to enhance the storytelling. I am including a few here to get you started. Once you do one, you will be hooked forever.

Today I talked to my children about dolls. I showed them how people made dolls before they could simply go to the toy store to buy one. They were entranced. I showed them how to make several kinds of dolls and, finally, how to make a doll from a sweet potato. Just add a bit of material; everyone can see that the potato already has eyes. And, I told them, if they looked close and used their imaginations, they could surely see the doll smile. The boys especially enjoyed making their dolls.

- Babies in a Cradle

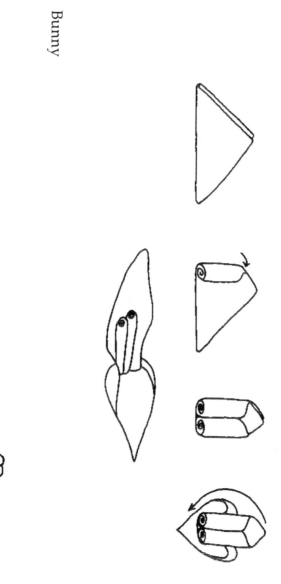

- Bunny

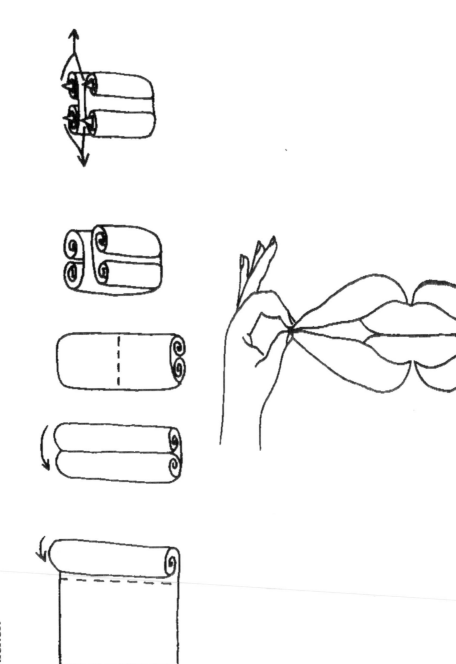

- Chicken

- Dolly

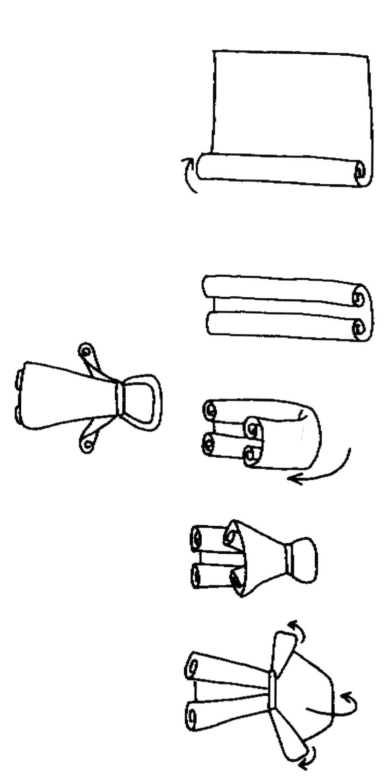

weaving

The enclosures for our lofts are made of farmer's cloth, a smooth but heavy wire. By tying ribbons, lace, and strips of material to the top hole in the "fencing," children can weave the entire loft. It doesn't matter if they skip holes or weave in a continuous direction. They help each other by poking and pulling the material through the holes. We also weave our cyclone fence outside with all the same materials as well as reeds, grasses, and other natural materials.

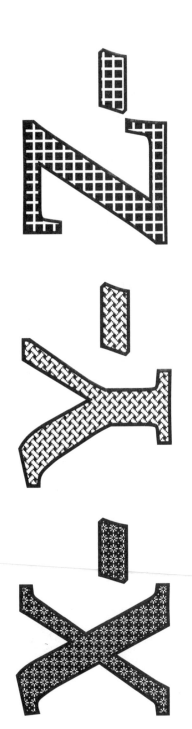

X x-rays

Y yarn

Z zest

x-rays

Obtain discarded X-rays from your local dentist, doctor, or hospital. When the children see how our bones are all alike no matter what we look like on the outside, there is a sense of uniformity and belonging.

yarn

Sometimes I give my children four or five balls of yarn about the size of softballs. They take them and tie the ends to a table leg or post and wander around the room, over and under things. Pretty soon, the whole room looks like a spider web. It makes it a bit difficult to get around the room for a day or two, but it's worth it for the coaction that occurs. The children pass the balls back and forth to each other. They drop them and roll them across the room. Sometimes they make elaborate plans about where to go.

zest

After reading all of these suggestions, perhaps you feel overwhelmed. None of these coacting activities can happen unless you bring a certain zest to whatever you do. Especially with children, we need to model that zest, that excitement about each new day.

One of the things that I always say when demonstrating something new at a workshop is "This is the best thing I've ever done!" Tomorrow there will be some other best thing. The most difficult thing for me to do is the thing I did last year: there are always so many new things to try. That's what keeps teaching alive for me and keeps it fun. I wish the same for you!

resources

Asch, Frank. *Bear's Bargain*. New York: Prentice Hall, 1985.

_____ and Vladimir Vagin. *Here Comes the Cat*. New York: Scholastic. 1989.

Aylesworth, Jim. *Mr. McGill Goes to Town*. New York: Henry Holt and Co., 1989.

Balian, Lorna. *The Aminal*. Nashville, Tenn.: Abingdon Press, 1985.

Bowers, Kathleen Rice. *At This Very Moment*. Boston: Little, Brown and Co., 1983.

Briggs, Raymond. *Jim and the Beanstalk*. New York: Coward-McCann, Inc., 1970

Bunting, Eve and Jan Brett. *Happy Birthday, Dear Duck*. New York: Clarion Books, 1988.

Cole, Joanna. *Anna Banana: 101 Jumprope Rhymes*. New York: Morrow Junior Books, 1989.

Douglass, Barbara. *Good as New*. New York: Lothrop, Lee and Shepard Books, 1982.

Two unlikely friends, a bear and a bird, caring enough about each other to help one another try to do the impossible, solve the problem.

"Don't believe anything you hear and only half of what you see," my mother always said. The Aminal speaks to this and teaches us that we have to experience things first hand.

Fox, Mem. *Wilfred Gordon McDonald Partridge*. Brooklyn, New York: Kane Miller Book Publishers, 1985.

The story of a young boy caring for an old person. My favorite book for helping children understand that when we get old, we still have the same human needs.

Fuchshuber, Annegert. *Giant Story/Mouse Tale: A Half Picture Book*. Minneapolis: Carolrhoda Books, Inc., 1982.

Gross, Theodore Faro and Sheila White Samton. *Everyone Asked About You*. New York: Philomel Books, 1990.

Heine, Helme. *Friends*. New York: Aladdin Books, 1986.

Heine gives us a sense of what friendship is all about, the joy, the outrageous fun, the fellowship.

———. *The Most Wonderful Egg in the World*. New York: Aladdin Books, 1987.

———. *The Pigs's Wedding*. New York: Aladdin Books, 1986.

Johnston, Tony. *Yonder*. New York: Dial Books, 1988.

Tony Johnston "sings" of families and friendships and caring.

Kraus, Robert. *Where Are You Going, Little Mouse?* New York: Greenwillow Books, 1986.

Robert Kraus always stresses the importance of family, caring, and helping.

Lyon, George Ella. *Come a Tide*. New York: Orchard Books, 1989.

A community pulls together during a time of natural disaster.

———. *Together*. New York: Orchard Books, 1989.

McKee, David. *Elmer*. New York: Lothrop, Lee and Shepard Books, 1968.

Friends go to extremes to make another friend feel all right about being different.

McPhail, David. *The Bear's Toothache*. Boston: Little, Brown and Co., 1972.

Morgan, Pierr. *The Turnip*. New York: Philomel Books, 1990.

Morris, Ann. *Hats, Hats, Hats, Hats*. New York: Lothrop, Lee and Shep ard Books, 1989.

_____. *Bread, Bread, Bread*. New York: Lothrop, Lee and Shepard Books, 1989.

Munsch, Robert. *David's Father*. Toronto: Annick Press, 1983.

_____. *50 Below Zero*. Toronto: Annick Press, 1986.

_____. *I Have to Go*. Toronto: Annick Press, 1987.

_____. *Millicent and the Wind*. Toronto: Annick Press, 1984.

_____. *Moira's Birthday*. Toronto: Annick Press, 1987.

_____. *The Paper Bag Princess*. Toronto: Annick Press, 1980.

Murphy, Jill. *Peace at Last*. New York: Dial Press, 1980.

Peek, Merle. *Mary Wore Her Red Dress and Henry Wore His Green Sneakers*. New York: Clarion Books, 1985.

Munsch's books are more significant and complex than many adults realize. He has spent time considering every word and page in relation to the needs and fears of children. I especially recommend the titles here for establishing a coactive atmosphere.

Polacco, Patricia. *The Keeping Quilt*. New York: Simon and Schuster, Inc., 1988.

Everyone has relatives who come to visit. This book acknowledges the fun and the crowded conditions that make for a special time.

Porter, Sue. *Little Wolf and the Giant*. New York: Simon and Schuster, Inc., 1989.

Rylant, Cynthia. *The Relatives Came*. New York: Bradbury Press, 1985.

Sandburg, Carl. *The Wedding Procession of the Rag Doll and the Broom Handle and Who Was in It*. San Diego:Harcourt Brace, 1967.

Seeger, Pete. *Abiyoyo: South African Lullaby and Folk Story*. New York: Macmillan, 1986.

Children working together and having great fun.

Spier, Peter. *Oh, Were They Ever Happy*. New York: Doubleday and Co., 1978.

Te Ata, told by, adapted by Lynn Moroney. *Baby Rattlesnake*. San Francisco: Children's Book Press, 1989.

Thompson, Richard. *Foo*. Toronto: Annick Press, 1988.

Wild, Margaret. *The Very Best of Friends*. San Diego: Harcourt Brace Jovanovich, 1990.

A moving lesson on death and friendship.

Wood, Donald and Audrey. *The Napping House*. Harcourt Brace Jovanovich. San Diego, 1984.

Thompson, Richard. *Foo*. Toronto: Annick Press, 1988.

Xiong, Blia, told by, adapted by Cathy Spagnoli. *Nine-in-One Grrr Grrr*. San Francisco: Children's Book Press, 1988.

on creating a coactive environment

Bos, Bev. *Before the Basics*. Roseville, California: Turn the Page Press, 1983.

_____. *Don't Move the Muffin Tins*. Roseville, California: Turn the Page Press, 1978.

Bredenkamp, Sue et al. *Developmentally Appropriate Practice in Early Childhood Programs Serving Children from Birth Through Age 8*. Washington, D. C.: National Association for the Education of Young Children, 1987.

Brown, Marc. *Hand Rhymes*. New York: E.P. Dutton, 1985.

Derman-Sparks, Louise and the A.B.C. Task Force. *Anti-Bias Curriculum: Tools for Empowering Young Children*. Washington, D.C.: National Association for the Education of Young Children, 1989.

Dowell, Ruth I. *Move Over Mother Goose*. Mt. Ranier, Maryland: Gryphon House, 1987.

All of these fingerplays can be adapted to be coactive.

Elkind David. *Grandparenting: Understanding Today's Children.* Grandview, Ill., Scott Foresman Co., 1990.

———. *The Hurried Child: Growing Up Too Fast Too Soon.* Reading, Mass.: Addison-Wesley, 1981.

Pellowski, Anne. *Family Story Telling Handbook.* New York: Macmillan, 1987.

———. *The Story Vine.* New York: Macmillan, 1984.

Williams, Sarah. *Round and Round the Garden.* New York: Oxford University Press, 1983.

Williams, Robert A. et al. *Mudpies to Magnets: A Preschool Science Curriculum.* Mt. Ranier, Maryland: Gryphon House, Inc., 1987.

Winslow, Marjorie. *Mud Pies and Other Recipes.* Yonker, New York: Pebble Press, 1961.

tapes

Bos, Bev et al. *Hand in Hand*. Roseville, California: Turn the Page Press.

_____. *Handed Down*. Roseville, California: Turn the Page Press.

_____ and Michael Leeman. *Thumbprints*. Roseville, California. Turn the Page Press.

Bos, Bev and Michael Leeman. *Thumbprints, Too*. Roseville, California. Turn the Page Press.

Chapin, Tom. *Family Tree*. A & M Records.

Hunter, Tom. *Bits and Pieces*. Bellingham, Washington: Long Sleeve Records.

_____. *The Tape of Our Record*. Bellingham, Washington: Long Sleeve Records.

_____. *Windows*. Bellingham, Washington: Long Sleeve Records.

Central themes in all of Tom Hunter's songs are caring for and sharing with other people.

index